NATALIE OSBORNE-THOMASON was born in Harpole, Northampton, England. A mother of three children and a natural psychic, she is an author, lecturer and researcher, and also gives personal readings. Since childhood she has been fascinated by the subject of ghosts, and has spent much of her spare time gathering information and first-hand experience. She has made numerous media appearances which include a feature in *The Daily Mail* and the television programmes *This Morning* (with Richard and Judy) and *Esther* (with Esther Rantzen). She is the author of *The Ghost-Hunting Case Book* and *Walking Through Walls*.

To

Gill...

Hope you enjoy

this one

Natalie

x x x x x

Natalie at Lesnes Abbey, London   Photo: Patrick Leonard

PSYCHIC QUEST

EPISODES FROM THE LIFE OF A GHOST HUNTER

NATALIE OSBORNE-THOMASON

CLAIRVIEW

For Mum and Dad,
to whom I will always owe so much.

Clairview Books
An imprint of Temple Lodge Publishing
Hillside House, The Square
Forest Row, East Sussex
RH18 5ES

www.clairviewbooks.com

Published by Clairview 2002

A catalogue record for this book is available from the British Library

ISBN 1 902636 34 1

Cover by Andrew Morgan Design
Typeset by DP Photosetting, Aylesbury, Bucks.
Printed and bound by Cromwell Press Limited, Trowbridge, Wilts.

Contents

Foreword

Writing this book has been a journey for me, a journey into the past involving tentative guesses as to the future. I was dismayed when, halfway through writing it, I fell awkwardly and broke my arm. However, this simply served to slow me down a little so that I could focus on my writing. Normally I concentrate on writing about other people, and I had not realized how difficult it would be to write about myself. I have written about the good and the bad in equal measure, for I feel that this is what life is all about. It is difficult to open oneself to what will effectively be the gaze of strangers, but on the other hand it has been a useful exercise since in writing about some of the more painful, embarrassing and upsetting aspects of my past I have been able to exorcise a few of my own 'ghosts'.

One thing I have tried to portray above all others is the evidence I have uncovered that points to survival after death and that there can be continued communication between us and those who have passed on from this life to the next. This theme has accompanied me throughout my life. I very much hope that people will enjoy reading this book and that it will help them open their minds a little to the wonderful things around them waiting to be discovered.

The subject closest to my heart has always been and will always be ghosts and hauntings. In uncovering the evidence one discovers real proof of the survival of the inestimable human spirit after death and, in the more common ways of recording, snippets of the past are literally brought back to life. In understanding more about ghosts one understands more about the human psyche, about our hopes and fears and what makes us tick.

My hope is that scientific advances in the near future will prove beyond doubt the existence of that other world which exists alongside and inside our own. Throughout history what seemed magical and mysterious became, when explained and verified scientifically, the facts of tomorrow's generation.

Above all I wanted this book to be one which would make readers stop and think about this life and what lies beyond it, and help them lose some of the fear of the mystery which surrounds and will perhaps always surround death.

I
EARLY EXPERIENCES

1

Small Beginnings

The classroom was hot and sticky, humid with the summer heat. A nondescript little man dressed in dusty grey overalls strode into the room and asked the teacher's permission to show us children a rat. It was dead and quite enormous, the largest specimen caught. 'Nearly as big as a small cat', the man told us with relish.

Our school was a small, yellow sandstone building on the edge of the village. We were soon to move to a new, bigger, purpose-built school when the old one closed, and we were all very excited. But for the moment our old school and its rodent problem proved a fascinating distraction. I was in my seventh year, a milestone year for me, as it turned out, a year of growing up, changing schools and the death of my grandmother, which was indirectly to set me on the path which I follow today.

Growing up in the pretty Northamptonshire village of Harpole was in some ways a mixed blessing. Nestling amid green fields it had been expanded greatly in the mid-1960s, with several developments of mostly redbrick dormer-style houses. Owing to the close and insular nature of a village community, even today people are not easily allowed any secrets, and past transgressions were not forgotten. There were always dens to discover, trees to climb and mischief to be

Photo: Patrick Leonard

The High Street, Harpole, Northampton, where I grew up

got up to by children with energy and time on their hands, but nevertheless Harpole was a safe place to grow up in. I was the middle child of three, and we lived in one of the new houses in the village. My elder sister Linnet, small and dark, was always described as the 'good' one. Kate, the youngest, with red hair and dark eyes, proved to be a precocious tomboy. I was normally described as the 'naughty' one, struggling with childhood *angst* yet having boundless energy and a drive which could not go unnoticed. (I have found this drive to be common with middle children.) These traits did not always mix harmoniously.

Our parents, Ken and Valerie Osborne, worked hard at the family business, so we children were often left to our own devices, which proved to be a good grounding in early independence. We could all cook and clean, for example. In the school holidays, however, I loved going to work with Mum, feeling the closest to her in character. My parents showed corporate films for companies and also worked as cinema projectionists.

I first found out about my grandmother being ill when I visited her in hospital. She seemed strangely sad and vacant, and Mum said she was just sad because Grandpa had died. Somehow she had lost the will to live. She had always been a plump and happy-looking old lady with twinkly blue eyes and a haze of curly grey hair. Now she just looked lost. I was only allowed to visit a few times before she got too ill. Refusing food and wanting to die, she had simply given up, hoping to rejoin her beloved husband. In the end I was told she had lost her sight, and then she gradually and painfully slipped away, weighing no more than four stone and barely making an impression in the bed. I shudder to think how my poor Mum coped, for she had been the youngest and her mother's favourite. I remember being told in hushed and tearful tones that my grandmother had 'gone'. I went to my room to let it sink in, and in bed that night I went to sleep uneasy and fretful.

When I woke up in the morning in the bottom bunk the sunlight was streaming through the curtains. Watching the motes of dust dancing in the air I rubbed my eyes to banish sleep. I felt a wonderful, warm presence and was at first at a loss to understand it. Then I noticed the figure. Small and gossamer-like, it seemed to be composed almost of vapour droplets, a bit like the effect when one sprays a perfume aerosol in the air. As I got used to the light I made out the shape. It was unmistakably my granny. I watched her for some moments and then she was gone, but the sense of happiness she had exuded remained. I skipped downstairs and wolfed down my breakfast. Everyone else in the house seemed upset, particularly Mum with her eyes red and swollen from crying. I told her not to be sad, 'Granny's OK, she's in the house with us.' Mum seemed cross at this and a little distracted. As far as my parents were concerned death was final; you simply didn't and couldn't come back.

I decided to wait for a better moment to bring the matter up, but a better moment never really came. My grandmother stayed with us for about two weeks. I only saw her image once more, but felt her presence more or less constantly over the days that followed. I had to pull my socks up and behave because I didn't want her to witness my usual naughty exploits teasing my sisters and cheeking my parents. I found it impossible to be sad at her death because I knew that she was alright; she was even fat again! Then one day I woke up and knew that she had gone, where to I was unsure, perhaps to the heaven that was sometimes talked about at school assembly.

The experience had a strong and fundamental effect on me and indeed it still does to this day, and it led me to have an unshakable belief in the survival of the 'spirit' or essence of a person at death. Indeed I very much doubt whether my interest in ghosts and mediumship would have flourished without this experience at such a young age.

Another influence on me at that time, and a strong one it seems, was that of my father. We never really got on too well when I was young, but I loved his stories. There was always a twist at the end, and the main character in the drama was usually a ghost or a monster. The setting tended to be an old house or castle far away from the rest of civilization. But he also sometimes took me to local haunted spots like the lane at Upton with its legend of a ghost that had scared horses in days gone by and made it impossible for travellers to progress after dark.

At about this time we took several holidays in Scotland, stopping at an assortment of old buildings ranging from farmhouse bed-and-breakfasts to castles. I have one vivid recollection of staying in an old house and having to share a room with one of my sisters. To the left of our bedroom door was a long corridor leading to the bathroom which was guarded by a suit of armour, its trusty axe in hand. Dad told us a story of how it came to 'life' at night when it would traverse the corridor chopping off the heads of any trespassers. I enjoyed this story, but as darkness fell and we were ushered off to bed I changed my mind. Waking up in the middle of the night and needing the toilet I crept to the door, opened it and peered out gingerly towards the bathroom door in the gloomy semi-darkness of the corridor. I was sure I saw the armoured figure move, ever so slightly. Scared, I ran back to bed and had to hang on until morning when the corridor had lost its sense of menace. It was on one of these holidays that I bought a book of Scottish ghost stories, and from then on I was hooked.

The next stage in my psychic development came about quite by accident when I was 13 or 14, during a summer day's riding trek with about six other people including a riding instructor, my mother and my sister Kate. It was a pleasant day with a blue sky, but the ground underfoot was quite wet

Aged 2, enjoying a boat trip!

and muddy. As we cantered en masse in fields near the Bramptons in Northamptonshire my pony Jamie, a chubby little roan, slipped in the mud and lost his footing, throwing me to the ground and then rolling on top of me. I was not aware of this at the time as I had been knocked out. Coming to my senses moments later I was convinced that I was in bed at home and had just woken up. All the events of that day were forgotten in that instant. Memory loss, however brief, is a most peculiar feeling and completely disorientating. With my mother's help I clambered back on to Jamie, bruised and mud-spattered, and we all rode home.

Looking back now I believe that this concussion and blow to the head directly precipitated a sort of psychic awakening with the accident acting like the turning-on of some kind of internal switch. A simple analogy is to imagine the brain as a kind of sophisticated radio set which has to be turned on if it is to receive signals or radio waves. When it is not turned on no information can be received. However, if the radio set were to be dropped on the floor the jolt might turn on the switch. Any head injury has the potential to do this too, but instead of radio signals the awakened brain receives messages either telepathically or as information from the past or the future.

It was some months after this that I saw my second ghost. I was walking with a boyfriend down one of the lanes in the village of Kislingbury. It was school disco-night held at the village hall, but being bored with the music we decided to go for a walk. It was quite late, and dark, but because the moon was almost full we were able to see quite clearly. Suddenly we heard a noise and there was a flash of orange light similar to a firework going off. We jumped, and there in the field was what I can only describe as an apparition. It was human-like but with eyes glowing red like hot coals in a fire. Terrified we rushed back to the safety of others at the disco. We never spoke of what we had seen but I had nightmares about it for a long time afterwards. A tangible sense of evil had emanated from the apparition. I now think this to have been a kind of 'low spirit entity' connected with that spot and dark deeds of the past.

My final years at secondary school passed quickly and as I was quite artistic, with drawing and painting my particular forte, I decided to go to college and study Fine Art, although I also loved English. I imagined myself one day earning a splendid living painting huge landscapes and portraits of the rich and famous. This was not to be, as is usual with ambitions. Within weeks of enrolling at Nene College of Art I was thoroughly bored.

The problem was that we students were left very much to our own devices, and as I had a well-developed lazy streak my work and enthusiasm suffered. The only class I really enjoyed was life-drawing, sketching and painting nudes. Indeed, some of my better sketches of feet and hands were sent to an exhibition. But this wasn't enough, and when I found out I was pregnant at the age of 17 by my long-term boyfriend Paul this came as something of a way out, giving me an excuse to leave, though I was admittedly also upset and disappointed.

My parents were naturally very upset and cross at my stupidity as I was considered the clever one of the family and they had high hopes for my future. Since I didn't really agree with abortion I decided it would be best to get married, forget any ambitions I might have and concentrate on the future of my

On my wedding day, aged 17 and still a child

baby. Looking back now I realize how childish I was at the time and unable fully to anticipate what a huge responsibility raising a child would be. I was little more than a child myself and still had a lot of growing up to do.

I had high hopes for my marriage and was determined to avoid the pitfalls experienced by my parents of constant arguments, overwork and only bumping into one another when they were tired and grumpy. With vivid memories of coming home from school when my parents were at opposite ends of the country I decided I wanted to be a stay-at-home mum. Although this decision to stay at home and bring up my children at least in their early years left me isolated, I felt in a way that it was right.

2

The Haunted Mill Cottage

The tall Chinese nurse placed the baby carefully into the clear perspex cot. 'Well, I must say you've got a real fighter here,' she said, smiling. 'It must have been all that Guinness!' It was early August 1983. I was 18 years old and had just given birth to my daughter Gemma. Pink, plump and perfect, she looked every inch a Botticelli cherub. The nurse had laughed when I had told her that I had religiously drunk a bottle of Guinness a day throughout the pregnancy. It was the only thing that had cured my anaemia, and I was sure it had helped my baby develop into the strong little infant in the cot next to my bed.

Home was a terraced cottage in the village of Bugbrooke. Within a few weeks of taking Gemma home I was beginning to get the hang of motherhood. We had been decorating the cottage bit by bit since moving in seven months earlier. The only room left to do and the one that filled me with dread was the attic bedroom. The cottage was on three floors with the two bedrooms on the top two floors. The problem was that since moving in I had felt the attic to be not quite right. It just had a bad feeling about it. Until then we had used it as a storeroom, and I had a strong seemingly irrational feeling that if I put the baby in that room something bad would happen to her. My husband Paul told me not to be so daft as it was a lovely large room ideal for a nursery. I even had some pink wallpaper from Laura Ashley ready for it, but try as I might I was unable to shake off the feelings. So I set up the cot on the upstairs landing and kept the attic door firmly shut.

Some months later the chance came up for our family to move to the larger house next door. So we began packing in preparation. About a fortnight before the move I was on my own in the cottage when I heard a strange noise coming from upstairs, sounding like something tapping on the attic room wall. Intrigued but a little scared I opened the door and looked in. The string of the light pull-switch was swinging violently on its own and the plastic toggle on the end was hitting the wall. Hence the noise. It was as if someone was standing a little way from the wall and pulling it fiercely again and again, letting it smash against the wall. Totally baffled, and at a loss as to what to do, I ran downstairs to get some scissors. I thought that cutting the string would be the only way to stop the noise. After that I felt glad to be moving next door away from whatever it was. It was to be only a short respite.

After Gemma's first birthday we went on a short holiday to Jersey. The island was beautiful with its small, rocky coves and golden beaches, and with a warmer climate than at home. In fact it was more like France than England, and a real treat. The hotel was nice, too; small and in the middle of the island.

On the second day of our holiday I had fed Gemma quite late and settled her down into the cot in our room. She fell asleep straight away, so I went downstairs to the television room to join Paul. Although this was easily within earshot of our room I went to check on the baby every 10 minutes or so. The news was on, and two other men were in the room, one engrossed in his paper. I picked up a book which another visitor had left behind, but had barely read a page when I heard a voice in my left ear. Scarcely above a whisper it said, 'The baby, check her, now!' I swung round. It was a woman's voice but I was the only woman in the room. Without thinking I grabbed the room key and raced up the stairs two at a time. My hands were shaking so much that I couldn't get the key into the lock. So I bent down and peered through the keyhole. What I saw filled me with horror.

Gemma was standing up in her cot with a plastic bag over her head. She was frantically trying to pull it off. Somehow the key slid in and I flew into the room, tearing off the bag. The baby's face was red and clammy and she was crying. Cuddling her in my arms I looked around, puzzled as to where the bag had come from. Under the cot was a small bin on its side. Someone had left it under the cot lined with a liner. She must have woken and found it. There and then I said a silent 'thank you' to whoever was looking after us. I realized then, as I had done all those years ago when my grandmother visited us, that there was more. Our actions and deeds are sometimes observed. Someone had been watching over Gemma that day, for sure.

My baby grew into a feisty little toddler over the next two years. Meanwhile I determined to nurture any potential psychic ability I might have. I was unsure at the time whether the voice that had saved my baby's life was a ghost, my own outwardly-projected subconscious or some kind of spirit guide or guardian angel. Like any new mother I was kept busy bringing up my daughter and running a home, but my interest in the spirit world grew. I feel sure that the learning process was encouraged by opening myself up to the possibility that I possessed some level of psychic, clairvoyant ability and also to the possibility that a spirit world existed seemingly alongside our own. This was very soon to be taken a stage further when, like Gemma, I had my very own brush with death.

3

Out of the Body

The bowl of the toilet was full of blood and floating in it was a small white foetus. I screamed both in physical agony and in shock. I had been staying for the day at my in-laws' house doing some decorating for them in the kitchen. They were away for a few days and it was to have been a surprise. My hands were still covered in white paint. I flushed the toilet. I couldn't bear to look, but part of me wanted to rescue the small scrap of life that was in the toilet. It felt wrong somehow simply to flush it away. Indeed, in the days that followed the miscarriage I wished that I had placed it in a little box and buried it.

Paul was visiting me in his lunch-hour and he called the doctor who told us to come in straight away. He was very kind, and after examining me told me I had been about 10 weeks pregnant. He sent me to hospital for a D&C after which I went home feeling much better. I was upset, but as I had not known that I was pregnant I had not had time to get used to it.

Two days later we were again at my in-laws' house and we were all on our way to chapel where my father-in-law, a retired Baptist minister, was preaching that night. As I walked down the street I suddenly came over all hot and clammy and my legs started to buckle. My brother-in-law told me I looked rough and should go back home. I barely made it back before being violently sick. Something was badly wrong, and I felt terrible. Paul took me back to the doctor who sent me back to hospital.

I had been in hospital for three days, vomiting constantly. The doctors thought I might have food poisoning and, as a precaution since it can be contagious, had put me in a room on my own. I was on a drip because I couldn't eat and had been so sick. I felt dreadfully weak. My mother had come to visit me early one evening and was sitting on the bed cuddling me. Two doctors came in and told us they wanted to operate that night as they now suspected either that I had suffered an ectopic pregnancy or there was something left inside causing an infection. Mum kissed me and promised to come back soon. A nurse told me she would be coming with my pre-med to ready me for the operation.

The room was quiet and quite dark with the curtains drawn. I remember feeling desperately ill and so weak. Looking over to the basin and mirror in the corner, I saw a cobweb hanging from the ceiling complete with spider. My body felt warm and floaty, and the next thing I knew I was looking in the mirror. My face seemed different, and the pain and nausea had gone. 'I'm better,' I thought, and turned round to look at the bed. It's hard to describe the shock I felt at seeing myself lying there, grey-faced and so still. Although I wanted to look away I couldn't, yet in myself I felt marvellous. The door opened and a nurse came in carrying a silver dish with a syringe. She spoke to me and then shook me gently when I did not respond. In an instant I was back; back in my bed and in pain. This was so quick and forceful that it was like a stretched elastic band snapping back.

I was well enough to leave the hospital a few days later, but it took me some months before I felt really well again. The doctors had warned me that I might not be able to have more children, but happily they were proved wrong. I had a son Laurie, followed 18 months later by another daughter, Becky.

In the seven years we spent in our second home odd paranormal events continued to happen regularly. The two older children shared an attic bedroom on the third floor, next to the bathroom. The atmosphere in this house seemed much better on the whole, but the light bulbs on the upstairs floor were forever blowing. And the top floor landing was permanently cold, despite the central heating. This landing ended in a blank wall to the next cottage where we had lived previously.

One morning Gemma came downstairs very upset and told us that after waking up in the night she had gone to the bathroom. She had seen a funny old lady sitting on the landing clutching her bedclothes. Gemma had grabbed her covers and the old woman had disappeared. Too frightened to go to the toilet, she had run back to bed and hidden under the bedclothes before finally falling asleep. Was that old lady just a child's vivid dream, or did the ghost, if that is what it was, somehow walk through the wall from next door? (In the past, when the cottages had been modernized, their internal structure and some walls had been changed.)

Once again we had an opportunity to go to a bigger house in the village, and as we now had three children we decided on a further move. The new house was lovely, an eighteenth-century cottage with a mature garden of about half an acre. Since having my last baby I had been suffering from ever-worsening post-natal depression. With three children under five I found myself constantly exhausted. In addition I began to suffer from insomnia and lost my appetite. Anyone who has suffered from the curse of depression will know how it can creep up on you slowly over a period of time until it has you firmly in its grip. Everything seems dark and hopeless.

Paul and my family tried to help and be sympathetic at first, but I found that people very soon lose patience with chronic depressives. No one wants to be close to misery, and most cannot understand why you cannot just hurry up and snap out of it. It's the loneliest illness of all, and looking back I can now see that it spelt the beginning of the end of my marriage. There were times when I felt so bad that I just wanted to go to sleep and never wake up. The only thing that kept me going and spurred me on at that time were my children. I realized, too, that just as we come into this world on our own we are, in many respects, alone in our battles through life. The only person one can ever trust totally is oneself. This was a hard lesson, but I knew that the only way out of the black hole I found myself in would be through my own efforts.

4

Feeling Blue

The room was grey; grey walls, grey ceiling, grey floor. Appropriate really, since anyone who ever came here must have felt grey inside as well. Lying on the metal hospital trolley I felt that this must surely be what hitting rock bottom was like. I was in one of the local mental hospital's electro-convulsive therapy rooms.

After struggling with spiralling post-natal depression and ever-worsening despair this is where I ended up. The kindly doctor told me that I was suffering from a serious bi-polar disorder or depressive illness. I had tried medication to no avail. A large part of the old Natalie, the person I considered myself to be, had vanished and been replaced by someone I could not and did not want to recognize: a sad, frightened individual. I remember how I sat crying in the doctor's office with my head in my hands when she recommended ECT. It was like being inside a bubble. No one could touch me or come near. I was separated from all humanity by this invisible wall. Years later I was to read *The Bell Jar* by Sylvia Plath, and realize that others, too, could feel this utter loneliness of suffering and torment.

I asked the doctor, 'Am I going mad?' This was my biggest fear, that I would lose my mind, but she just smiled gently and said, 'Don't worry. The very fact that you worry for your sanity means that you are certain not to lose it. Truly mad people are always sure that they are sane.' This thought kept me going in the weeks that followed. Over a period of six weeks I had twelve ECT treatments. As with everything, the first time was the worst. I had little faith at the time that it could make me better. I was only 24 and had little faith in anything. I felt that my world was in pieces. I remember having to lie on the trolley and being told not to worry. An injection into the back of my hand made me feel heavy and drowsy. Hearing a noise I glanced to the left and saw someone else who had been wheeled in to wait for the treatment; a poor, frightened creature of about 60 who appeared to be trying to push the nurses away in a desperate bid to escape. Her dark eyes were moist with tears and her shaking limbs bone-thin and scrawny.

Waking up some time later I felt confused and, as I had been warned, I had a headache to end all headaches. A nurse brought me a cup of tea and encouraged me to sit up. Mum was there and gave me a hug. She had been very much against my having the treatment as it frightened her, but I believe that at the time it was my only hope. A downside of this treatment is that it induces memory loss, and I found that I retained only patchy memories of the previous three years, but luckily as time passed most of them have returned, though occasionally I still suffer blanks.

Mum took me home that day where I went to bed as advised to sleep off the effects of the anaesthetic. Gemma was at school and my mother-in-law was looking after the two younger ones. I got up in the afternoon feeling strangely numb and wandered downstairs. Paul arrived back briefly from work to see how I was. I remember asking him how I looked, and he replied,

'Shocking, actually!' It was typical of him to try and use a joke to defuse the situation. True gallows humour. With new tablets to take and lithium to stabilize me I gradually got better, but it took a long time. For every little bit of progress I made there were also setbacks. I also had counselling, and slowly the blackness receded.

After going through all this I realized the truth in the saying: What doesn't kill you makes you stronger. There is a tendency to see people who have suffered breakdowns and depression as somehow weak; weaker than others who have mercifully been spared that fate. But this is not true. To come through a major illness infuses you with a sense of your own achievement and potential, and hopefully also gives you an enduring compassion for the sufferings of others. Another common reaction to mental illness of any type is shame and embarrassment. Family and friends may not want or even find themselves able to talk about the 'trouble' their loved one is in. Paul, in fact, gave me strict instructions not to talk about it as no one would understand. I felt ashamed at the time, and even now it is difficult to write about these things. But I have learnt not to worry too much about what others will think. If we can talk and be open about these things perhaps one day many of the taboos associated with mental illness will disappear. These feelings are largely born out of fear, the same basic fear that surrounds death in our culture. If it is hidden away and not spoken about it won't happen to 'us'.

My illness made me determined to find some purpose and meaning for my life, a general plan and direction to follow. This decision was to bring about a total change for myself and my family, and a yearning for a greater understanding of the world of ghosts that had so captured my imagination as a child. It was my battle with depression that ultimately brought with it a greater understanding of myself and empathy for the suffering and anguish of others. This was to prove invaluable for my work in the future.

5

Walking through Walls

Slowly the cloak of depression lifted, although dark moods I found difficult to deal with still sometimes took me by surprise. Many things helped me: my family (although unfortunately Mum and Dad were by now divorced), my beautiful garden, living in a house I loved, and my books. But for a long time after the illness and the ECT I felt like a vase that had been shattered and then stuck back together, so I worried that I might fall apart at any moment. I began to paint again, which was good, but I so much longed to write. Little did I know that my inspiration would come literally from quite close to home.

On moving into our new house beside the river we had all felt it to have a very pleasant atmosphere. Made from local yellow sandstone that had mellowed over two centuries, it sat overlooking the cricket field and the stream which gives the village of Bugbrooke its name. Once again I sensed a presence and wondered whether perhaps this house, too, was haunted. We didn't have long to wait for the first incident. Over the seven years we lived there many supernatural episodes occurred, too many to put down to chance, and witnessed by numerous people.

Since the garden was quite large and I was struggling to cope with it, I had put an advert in the local shop for a gardener to come for a few hours per week. Driving up to the house one afternoon after shopping I noticed an elderly lady standing in the garden. She appeared deep in thought and had bent down to smell a rose. I parked the car thinking that she must have come about the gardening job but was surely a bit too old; I also felt a bit cross at her rudeness in simply letting herself in like that. As I walked across the lawn I was then astonished to find she had vanished. I searched the garden but there was nowhere for her to have gone without first passing me and the car. In my mind I was going over exactly what I had seen when it hit me that the woman in the garden, looking larger than life in her tweed skirt and sensible leather shoes, was Mrs Tievens who had lived in our house before us but had since died from cancer. Feeling a little shocked I went inside; it seemed impossible, yet I knew what I had seen.

Other incidents over the ensuing months confirmed to me that something strange was going on. Years later I was to receive confirmation of a sort from a scientist to back up my claims, but for the present it all seemed a puzzle, one that I was at a loss to solve or explain.

I remember another occasion when a friend and I were sitting just chatting on sofas directly opposite one another. All of a sudden we both jumped as a shadowy figure traversed the room from the door beside us and crossed directly between us before disappearing by the fireplace. It was semi-transparent and indistinct, but we both saw it. Taken aback, we forgot what we had been discussing and went into the kitchen. Talking about it, we both described the apparition in identical ways, but funnily enough we were at a loss as to whether it had been male or female.

The most common phenomena were strange noises, and on

many occasions when I was alone in the house and the children were all at school I heard footsteps or marbles rolling along a wooden floor. There was also another sound which, however, proved to have a mundane solution. If you stood in the kitchen when it was windy you could hear a moaning and sighing noise that sounded all too human. Sometimes it rose to a crescendo of awfulness, resembling what I imagined the moans of the infamous Irish wailing banshee to be like. My mother was scared when she first heard it, exclaiming, 'Whatever in the world was that?' I discovered the answer to this mystery when I was up a ladder cleaning the porch windows and noticed a loose tile on the porch roof with the corner chipped off. This must have created a wind-tunnel effect, and we did indeed only hear that noise when the weather was exceptionally windy.

In my investigations in many haunted locations since then I have sometimes found equally mundane explanations behind phantom sounds. This can be a disappointment, of course, but to others it is a relief. One must always try and rule out natural building accoustics on an investigation. This incident in my own home proved a valuable lesson.

My little sister Kate had emigrated to Melbourne, Australia, and Gemma and I were fortunate enough to take a holiday there together. It was during those few weeks away from my at times bizarre home environment that I decided to write a book about my own experiences and those of others like myself.

I knew that I would have to start knuckling down if I was to write, but what to write and how to begin were the two questions playing on my mind. I had recently read a book by the veteran ghost-hunter Peter Underwood, and I wrote to him asking to join the Ghost Club. This is a London-based group that meets regularly to investigate hauntings, often spending the night in those locations. They also hold monthly meetings at the Savage Club in London with the guest speaker usually a writer on the supernatural. My application was successful and I set about studying my chosen subject. Being such a bookworm I had read extensively already, both fact and fiction. I was also a subscriber to the 'magazine of the strange and anomalous', *The Fortean Times*, and I decided to place an advert asking for people who had experienced hauntings to contact me.

The project mushroomed and soon took on a life of its own. Many people contacted me, and after separating the wheat from the chaff (some of the letters were from real crackpots and cranks) I had a starting point. Our local paper *The Chronicle & Echo* ran a piece about me, and lots of contacts in my home county of Northamptonshire arose from this.

My first ever interview was with the landlord of The Griffin, a public house in the small town of Higham Ferrers. The pub dates back to the thirteenth century and is very quaint with its inglenook fireplace and oak-beamed ceiling. The landlord took me on a tour, telling me about the ghosts. One is thought to be the victim of a rape during the Civil War. She wears a blue velvet dress and is usually seen by the fireplace. The pub has also been the victim of a poltergeist-like attack which occurred in the mid-1980s. For instance the jukebox would suddenly come on by itself and play 'In the Summertime' in the middle of the night. Very annoying, and it was always the same tune. Objects, usually socks, would go missing only to reappear in bizarre places. I soon found out that lots of pubs lay claim to having a resident ghost. Perhaps this could be due to their great age, and also to the fact that pubs were often used as a makeshift morgue for laying out the dead, especially in rural areas where they were often the only public building.

I also received letters and phone calls from people whose homes were haunted. Often the severity of the disturbance was much exaggerated, but I visited them all. Paul got fed up as he couldn't understand my new-found interest, and he dismissed my writing ambitions as daft. His scepticism simply served to spur me on since being a stubborn Taurean I don't take much notice of other people's opinions. The book *Walking through Walls* took me two years to write and reported on 50 cases, most of them local.

My family assumed that I would be satisfied now, and forget all about the ghost-hunting, but of course I had become totally bitten by the bug. I sincerely felt that I was uncovering some answers to the mystery of 'ghosts' and with that also finding some proof of life after death. The experiences I had had (seeing the ghost of my grandmother twice, the old woman in the garden, and my brief out-of-body excursion) helped me as well. I also felt a strong desire to help others make sense of ghostly encounters and show them they weren't going mad and that their's was a common experience with a long history that crossed all cultural boundaries. Sometimes I simply wanted to listen, and I quickly realized that I needed to tackle a much larger project, a more in-depth work involving some of the answers I had uncovered along the way.

I was to be fortunate in meeting many wonderful and interesting people on my journey, individuals who helped me often at great cost to themselves in both time and advice.

But not all the people I have met on my journey thus far have been so pleasant. Lurking on the fringes of this field are also the sharks, charlatans and individuals who, for want of a better word, appear to be downright evil. The paranormal, like any other phenomenon on the very edges of society, attracts a real mix of interested parties both good and bad.

With hindsight I see that when I first set out on my path I was naïve, unquestioningly trusting those who offered help without realizing that they might have ulterior motives. But life is there to live and to learn lessons which, if you fail to learn, you merely fail – full stop.

6

Three Types of Ghost

Before I began to study the phenomenon of 'ghosts' I thought that all ghostly experiences could be lumped together as being all pretty much the same. How wrong I was! I soon realized that for investigative purposes at least there were three main categories, namely the 'stone tape-recording' type, the spirits of the dead, and poltergeists, and I came to have personal experience of all three. I have listed them in the order of their frequency. The largest group seems to occur in as much as three-quarters of all reports. Spirits make up the next largest group, while classic poltergeist infestation is the rarest. Of course there are other small sub-groups such as the *doppelganger* or ghosts of the living, ghosts of animals and even of inanimate objects, but these can usually fit under the umbrella of one of the three main groupings.

Over the past century many eminent writers have commented on the fact that some spectral appearances seem to fit in with what is known as the 'stone tape-recording' theory. Just as we can trap the images and sounds of living people on videos and films so, possibly, were the actions and sounds of long-dead people trapped and recorded by some as yet not understood mechanism. It seems that stones and bricks may act as primitive recording equipment when the conditions are right. Thus a young man saw Roman legionaries tramping along at the level of the old Roman road in York. There have been scores of sightings in which a spectre is seen always performing the same tasks or actions, like a piece of film set in an almost everlasting loop played out again and again for generations.

The lady I saw in my garden at Bugbrooke would probably fit into this category. Her appearance involved no interaction between herself and the viewer; indeed, it would almost appear to be pointless and serve no purpose. Another example of this type is the grey lady who haunts the Royal Theatre in Northampton. She has usually been sighted in the evenings and on one occasion actually walked straight through a man who had been working late at the theatre and followed her, enquiring as to who she was and what she wanted. Her solid, totally realistic appearance prevented the man from thinking for one moment that she might be a ghost.

My initial research for *Walking through Walls* involved mostly letters concerned with such ghosts. I think that the reason why they are so common is in part connected with the high prevalence of old, period properties in Britain, as well as our bloody and often terrible history. (Strong emotions seem to be a part of the equation.) The right atmospheric conditions are also needed, thus damp and humid or muggy weather seems to precede encounters in most instances.

Spirits are the traditional ghosts of old. These are what we immediately think of when asked to consider what is a ghost. Seeing the figure of my grandmother so shortly after her death would fit into this category. In fact my research has shown that most of these ghosts are seen by a loved one or family member in the two weeks following a death. I do not know why there is this short time-frame of opportunity. Perhaps for those two weeks or so the person's spirit remains on the earthly plane before moving on, because many of us die before we are really ready and have, in a sense, unfinished business and this is a time for us to sort out our affairs. For those left behind it is also a time of acute and tangible grief, as well as the funeral and all that involves. Sceptics might be inclined to argue that any sightings at this time should be written off as mere hallucinations brought on understandably by wanting to see once more the person who has died. However, this does not explain even a small number of all the cases. Frequently the ghost of a person is seen who is not yet known to be dead. There was a plethora of such instances during the two world wars. Because of the slowness of the post it often took many days for the bereaved to receive notification, but when the fateful letter finally arrived the distressing news was already known. In my years of searching for ghosts I have found this type of sighting to be much more common than I would have believed.

Another incident happened to a good friend who had a very vivid dream about her cat lying badly injured by the side of the road. On waking up she knew the information to be true and she did not have to wait long for confirmation. Someone had found the nearly dead cat and taken him to a vet who traced my friend. With surgical care the cat eventually got better although his eye had been badly hurt. Telepathic communications which take place at times of severe illness, near death or actual death point to evidence that human emotions such as love, fear and even hate can be passed from one person to another regardless of distance. Human and even animal consciousness is tremendously powerful.

Without exception, all those I have interviewed who have seen a loved one after death have felt themselves to have benefitted in the long run even if at the time they were frightened or shocked. Something so positively beneficial should not be dismissed lightly.

Poltergeist hauntings, which can be described as a kind of infestation, are much rarer. I remember as a young girl seeing a programme about the Enfield poltergeist case on TV. The focus of the outbreak appeared to be Janet, the pubescent daughter of Mrs Harper, a single parent who struggled valiantly for months against a veritable onslaught of supernatural phenomena which were witnessed and recorded by eminent researchers who included Maurice Grosse and the writer Guy Lyon Playfair. The small council property was subjected to spontaneous movement of objects, levitation of Janet and a cushion, strange noises and, most dramatically of all, the seeming possession of Janet. She would enter trance-like states and emit a dead, guttural growl which turned into the voice of an old man. He told them he was a man who used to live in the house. Some bizarre, almost evil energy appeared to be using Janet's vocal cords to air its own grievances. The experts who recorded Janet in action felt it would be almost impossible for her to be making these sounds herself. I was about the same age as Janet when I saw all this on TV, and I felt strongly for her. I had a sense of empathy and shock that an innocent person could be invaded like that. It scared me, for the voice sounded evil and intent on having its own way at whatever cost to the girl's physical and mental well-being.

It made me consider the power of spiritual attack. Looking back on it now, with the benefit of all I have learnt through my own research, I realize that the Enfield case was unusual in that it combined elements of all three types of haunting. There was the possible spirit of someone who had died (the old man's voice), the 'recording' element in the spontaneous noises (possible sounds from the house's past), and typical poltergeist effects such as the disruption and movement of objects with possession. The unusual multi-layered nature of the case and also its duration marked it out as special.

Little did I know when watching the Harper's dramatic homelife that my own adult life would be affected by poltergeist-like haunting. Whilst living in the cottage at the western end of Bugbrooke I experienced all manner of small poltergeist-like effects over the years. Taken separately they were perhaps insignificant, but cumulatively they told their own story. Some people appear to attract ghostly activity throughout their lives to a greater or lesser extent. Many others whom I have interviewed have told me a similar story. Usually they are creative, artistic types. Poltergeist hauntings generally require a focus personality, feeding off their energy to manifest effects. Perhaps part of the energy is typical teenage *angst* or, in an adult focus, frustration, depression or anger such as I have experienced on occasions. This could explain why such hauntings seldom occur in happy, totally harmonious households where there is no negative energy to work with. Whether the actual 'poltergeist' (German for 'noisy spirit') is a separate, thinking entity or more simply some strong psychokinetic energy force, or a combination of both, I am still unsure. One thing I am sure of, however, is that such hauntings are very real and can happen to anyone. They are distressing in the extreme.

7

The Incredible Electric Woman on TV

As I became more involved in my personal study and quest for ghosts and finished my first book, I realized that to find new cases I needed publicity. The local paper *The Chronicle & Echo* ran an article on me, and from this I met my good friend Patrick Leonard who from then on helped me on overnight ghost vigils and with interviewing witnesses and photographing scenes of haunted locations and people all over the country. It was nice to find someone who understood my love of the paranormal world.

My search for publicity for my work soon snowballed and at times, I'm afraid, bordered on the farcical. But I made good contacts, one of whom was the maverick scientist Albert Budden. I was very nervous about my first foray into the world of television (on Channel 4's Big Breakfast programme), spending the night before going over and over what might go wrong. I was to talk about the bizarre effect I have on electrical equipment. *The Sun* newspaper had published a story about me in which I had mentioned to a journalist that I was unable to wear a watch because it would always stop or lose time. Sometimes I affected household items such as the TV, vacuum cleaner, iron etc. I would try and use one of these only for it to malfunction or even explode. This happened in cycles and I linked it to the haunting in our cottage and the poltergeist-like goings-on.

The problem seemed to be mainly focussed on me and was annoying in the extreme and, of course, over the years expensive. We had to buy numerous TVs and irons, and light-bulbs didn't last five minutes. We had the wiring in our house checked and it was found to be safe. In the end I got used to these bizarre incidents, but at times they were embarrassing, and I was surprised that the media found all this so interesting. On the show I was to be tested by Albert, who is an expert on electro-magnetic pollution and its effects on the human body. He suspected that I might be suffering from something called electro-magnetic hypersensitivity.

At an unearthly hour of a winter's morning I was driven to the studio, not knowing precisely what to expect. Albert introduced himself to me in the waiting area. His hand-shake was firm and he seemed very friendly. We had a few minutes to chat before going on air and he asked me a series of questions from a standard list which he used to discover whether a subject was 'electrically hypersensi-tive' which was assumed to be the case if a person answered 'Yes' to many of the questions. One I remember was, 'Do you consider yourself to be psychic?' This made me laugh because I didn't just consider this to be the case; I knew, with good reason, that I was psychic. Another question was, 'Have you ever been struck by light-ning or received a severe electric shock?' I had indeed received such a shock from a frayed connection on an old sewing machine; it had thrown me to the floor. But I for-got all about the ECT treatment which, of course, would have had a more sustained effect. Albert thought that the sewing machine could have triggered the condition.

Then we were ushered into the live studio where the presenters interviewed us. I had hoped to be able to talk about my book; in fact, this was my only reason for participating. However, the piece was very short and the presenters were only interested in the strange things that happened to me in connection with electrical equipment. I was treated as a bit of a freak and even Albert was not taken seriously; they couldn't even spell his name properly. A new iron, of all things, was presented to me since I had blown up so many, and we were ushered off like a pair of naughty schoolchildren. This experience nearly put me off going on TV for good but, as I correctly presumed, things could only get better.

After my TV debut, Albert and I telephoned each other quite frequently, and we have since ended up together on several TV shows. For over 15 years he has been researching all aspects of the paranormal, from UFOs to ghosts. He started out as a believer but has since changed his views. He now considers that all paranormal experiences can be put down to the effects of our modern world which has become polluted with invisible electric and magnetic fields. These cause ball-plasma UFOs and trigger hallucinatory effects in susceptible people, leading to sightings of ghosts and aliens. I disagree with Albert on this, as I believe that real psychic ability does exist and is even common, and that ghost sightings can be genuine. But I felt his contribution to be an important one that could provide a piece of the puzzle which I wanted to construct. I had thought for a long time that there was indeed an important electrical component to ghosts and psi abilities and that psychics were picking up electrical signals from the environment and reading them subconsciously. Ghosts, on the other hand, seemed to utilize the ambient heat and often also the electrical current from appliances in a room in order to appear or move objects. It seemed that the two of us were at opposite ends of the problem, each being convinced of the validity of our own beliefs. Albert sought to use his research to explain away all hauntings in scientific terms, while I felt that his theory merely covered the effects often found in poltergeist outbreaks.

Albert and a German film crew 'Pro 7' came to my house at Bugbrooke later that year to film a short piece for German TV. The item called me the 'Elektro-Frau' and recounted many of the phenomena. After this, Albert told me about the Canadian physicist Hutchinson and showed me a video of his work. In the 1980s Hutchinson had created a huge machine using a mishmash of equipment which generated large opposing electrical and magnetic fields. He was amazed at the strange effects this exerted over a random selection of objects placed in the vicinity. Small bowls levitated, planks of wood stood on end all by themselves, and yoghurt slurped out of a pot. Even fairly large metal objects were moved by an invisible force, many of these remaining permanently bent. Spontaneous fires broke out and sparks flew in the laboratory. This might seem to belong to the world of fiction, but there it is, captured on video for all to see. Hutchinson had created in his lab many of the manifestations found in a poltergeist outbreak simply by combining the two forces of electricity and magnetism in a previously unknown way. I had read of Hutchinson's work in *The Fortean Times*, but to see this video was a real eye-opener.

Perhaps humanity as a whole is unwittingly conducting a similar experiment with all our new technology. Surrounded as we are by high-tension cables, microwave transmitters, radio masts, mobile phone masts, not to mention all the electrical appliances we have in our homes, we surely have a veritable sea of invisible electro-magnetic fields coursing through our bodies, in some instances causing physical illnesses and in others making the conditions right for ghosts, either poltergeist outbreaks or heightened levels of psychic ability which enable individuals to see apparitions. This is the crucial point on which I differ from Albert Budden, for what he regards as hallucinations in those susceptible to these fields I regard as real sightings, especially for example in cases where the identical apparition is witnessed over the years by numerous different people who have had no prior contact with one another. A different effect of these fields is physical illness, particularly disorders of the glands, thyroid, pancreas, adrenals and so on, which is perhaps not too surprising since these parts of our anatomy are highly sensitive to toxins of any kind. Albert was not surprised when I mentioned my own recent health problems with hypothyroidism and adrenal malfunction. He also pointed out that some individuals absorb large amounts of electricity in their body which is then discharged in short bursts. This is what affects the electrical equipment used by such sufferers.

It was around this time that offers for TV appearances began to trickle in, such as This Morning with Richard and Judy, and Esther Rantzen's afternoon chat show. Both of these featured Albert's ideas quite strongly, although on the Esther show his radical views were shouted down by another veteran researcher, Maurice Grosse, who had been involved in the Enfield case which had fired my imagination as a child. There were to be many more radio and TV appearances. It seemed as though media interest in the paranormal was tied up in some kind of pre-millennium *angst*. As for my small part in it, I was quite happy to be swept along on the tide.

8

Preventing a Car Crash

For about six months I had been coming to rely more and more on my psychic impressions and as a result felt my ability growing. The following incident is true, but I still find it incredible and hard to believe.

On a very wet and miserable day in late 1996 I happened to meet two very interesting people in a large and busy café at Euston railway station in London. (Because of the sensitive nature of the case I have changed the names.) Clive runs a busy show-business agency and Simon is one of his clients, an actor and theatre comedian. As we sat drinking coffee and chatting, Simon told me he had seen an article about me a few weeks earlier in one of his wife's magazines. The article was about electro-magnetic hypersensitivity and psychic powers. I remembered it as having been rather silly and exaggerated, so I was embarrassed when he mentioned it.

Clive then jokingly grabbed my hand. (As I do palm-reading I always notice people's hands and feel that the lines on them are like a unique map showing our lives past and present. This map can be de-coded, and the information it represents can be acted on. Of course this does not mean that our future is set in stone. I liken it more to a firm jelly which can be subtly pushed around and changed. The lines on the map are there at birth as a guide to our potential.)

I noticed from Clive's hand that he had a child and that his wife was pregnant, and told him as much. He was taken aback. I gave him a few other details of his life, and said that someone named Louise would very much like him to call. Then Simon asked me to read his palm. He was a bit sceptical and his was more complex. I picked up that he had almost died once from suffocation, which he confirmed had happened during his days as a North Sea diver. I also sensed that his baby daughter was in hospital suspected of having a serious genetic illness, and that she would very soon be alright. (Indeed, a few days later she had improved and went home. The illness had been a false alarm.)

Then I heard a voice, clear despite being a whisper in my left ear. It was a man's voice and it said, 'Please tell Clive not to drive his car; he could get killed today. I don't want him to get into his car, it's too dangerous.' I knew this was a spirit voice, but I felt astonished nevertheless and didn't quite know what to say. Could I be mistaken, or had I imagined it? Somehow I felt that I must at least attempt to warn Clive about his car. But what to say? So I blurted out, 'You're not planning on going any-where by car later today by any chance, are you? Because there's something very wrong with your car. Get rid of it.' Putting things gently has never been my strong point, and I did feel foolish, especially when the two men insisted that Clive's car was fine, being quite new. Simon had a gig later that day and so the two would be having to travel down to Brighton. They had no choice. However, a bit freaked by the accuracy of my other information they reassured me that they would have the vehicle checked out at the nearest garage. We said goodbye, promised to keep in touch, and went our separate ways.

At lunchtime the next day I received a call from a very excited showbiz agent. The pair had gone to the nearest garage after our meeting, not thinking for one moment that my information might be correct, but just to make sure. After checking the car the mechanic had told them that it was in a lethal condition. The brakes were faulty and there was a six-inch nail in one of the front tyres which would probably have resulted in a blow-out – not a good prospect on a busy motorway.

Clive told me over and over again how grateful he was, as he believed that I had saved both their lives that day. Then he asked how in the world I had known about his car when he hadn't suspected anything. So I told him of the whisperer. There followed a rather stunned silence and then he told me that his good friend Tony had died in a car crash only months before. We both realized that it had been Tony's voice, and it gave us goosebumps.

About two weeks later I was in London again, so I dropped in at the agency to see how they were getting on after their escape. Walking into the small building near to the railway bridge I sensed at once that it was haunted. It was being haunted by Tony, and his presence was mostly in the back corner by the coffee machine. I informed Clive of my suspicion, and a young secretary who overheard our conversation went white. She, too, had felt a coldness and presence next to the drinks machine and was a little afraid.

Hoping to confirm the identity of the ghost, and as a kind of test, Clive said, 'See if you can pick out my friend from these photos.' There were six. I think the others were of his clients. One photo seemed to leap out at me, so I chose it, and it was of

Tony. I believe now that I was meant to meet those two men that day if for no other reason than to warn them of the hidden danger they both faced. Perhaps the dead man had tried to contact his dear friend but could not make himself heard. His kind spirit could not bear the thought of Clive facing the same awful fate.

I was once given a definitive description by a mischievous spirit of exactly how mediumship works. I was roundly told off and warned not to get big-headed, since spirits regarded us psychics as nothing more than working telephone boxes. Most people are like broken-down phone boxes: no communication is available. Spirits are always relieved to find an available medium to make the connection. After all, there is nothing more frustrating than wanting to phone a friend or loved one when the phone box doesn't work or has been vandalised.

The information which comes my way is usually of a far more trivial nature, which comes as a slight relief. Around this time a young woman came to visit me at home for a psychic reading. She seemed very nervous and agitated, and when I looked I saw a vision of blood. But I was told, 'Tell her not to worry, the blood is not bad.' When I related this message she smiled and looked more relaxed. For about a year she had been suffering from hepatitis contracted while on holiday abroad. I was able to reassure her that she would recover. She was relieved, since she had worried about liver damage and the doctors were unsure of its possible effects.

9

Searching for Answers

The next two years were a time of great change in which my marriage came to an end and I wrote my next book. My sister Kate also went through a marriage break-up, and to get away for a few days we decided to spend a long weekend in New York.

There was a reason why I wanted to visit New York over and above the usual touristy one. Ever since I could remember, but especially since becoming an adult, I had been aware of having a spirit guide, a protective influence in my life, but I only came to appreciate her fully when I grew up. She is a woman named Vera who lived in the Brooklyn area of New York where she worked as a nurse. She told me she had died before I was born in a swimming accident by hitting her head on the bottom of the pool. She had been quite young. I have always felt an affinity with America and Americans, and perhaps this is why. We all have such guides who help and assist us in life, but it is up to us to choose to listen and take notice of them and all the subtle cues they give us. I hope to return to New York one day and try to find where Vera lived and worked and why she chose me. Perhaps our personalities are similar, but I don't know.

I have seen her only once, when I was ill in hospital with an infection. I was in a great deal of pain and woke up to find a nurse seated by my bed patting my hand. Her uniform was strange and unlike any the other nurses were wearing, but this didn't register with me until afterwards. She was middle-aged and slim, with glasses and tight curly hair. I asked her whether I was going to be alright, and she told me I would be, and not to worry. When I woke up again after falling asleep once more I felt much improved. When a woman in the bed opposite asked how I was feeling I told her I was much better and that my visitor must have cheered me up. She asked, 'What visitor?' and said she had seen none since the day before.

The year of the divorce was terrible. I moved into a new house with the children while Paul stayed in the old one as it was a tied cottage that came with his job. The new house was barely half the size of the old one, and I missed the garden dreadfully. We all felt cramped together and on top of one another, but the arguments being only between myself and the children were easier to bear. I knew it would be hard on my own, but I felt this would be preferable to being half of a very dysfunctional couple.

My health at that time was bad partly due, I suppose, to all the stress. The children were what kept me going, together with my writing and ghost-hunting. Albert Budden helped me find a new publisher, so I had to keep busy and find new cases and investigations. I was also kept quite busy with palmistry and tarot card readings. Curiously, I have found over the years that my psychic and mediumistic abilities are strongest when I am at a low ebb physically, and other psychics and mediums I have met also suffered badly with their health. Perhaps these abilities are one of the body's senses. It is well-known that when a person loses one of the senses all the others sharpen up to compensate.

This was demonstrated to me once when I read the palm of a blind lady. It was the most difficult reading I have ever had to do. As I sat down beside her she told me sternly not to be nervous. I wondered how she could tell as she couldn't even see me, and of course her words had the opposite effect and I was a bundle of nerves. I felt she could sense everything about me and was a shrewd judge of character. What I had to tell her seemed quite impressive to me. She had been brought up by nuns abroad and had not always been blind but had become so following an illness. As I started to relax a little I let my mind wander and spoke out loud the faint impressions I was picking up. This is something I try to do at all of my readings, however bizarre the images that come into my head. I feel that in doing this I am picking up aspects of the person's thoughts and personality. In this case there was something about a baby crocodile. 'Oh, that,' she said. 'Yesterday my husband drove past a building that used to be his favourite restaurant where they had a tank with baby crocodiles. He was upset because it's now a launderette.' She gripped my hand tightly, her blank eyes staring straight ahead. 'But I'm not interested in him, I want you to tell me about me.' I couldn't help but laugh. Although I left little impression on that woman she had greatly impressed me. Her senses rivalled anything I possessed yet this was entirely normal for her.

Interesting phenomena continued to dog my path. One incident springs to mind which I still find baffling. Early one evening I was typing up some notes about a case that in some ways mirrored the peculiar phenomenon of spontaneous human combustion. It concerned a young girl who was suffering badly from period pains. One night she was walking with her friend past a cemetery when her body started to emit bright red sparks. Her first instinct was to run and the pair ran home only to find that the phenomenon had stopped. I was writing this up, taking advantage of the quiet house while the children were out with their father. The phone rang, making me jump and I accidentally pressed the wrong keys on my typewriter. After answering the phone I returned to my work. Glancing at the page I noticed my mistake. There at the end of the sentence was the number 666! I corrected the page and continued.

Five minutes later the children returned with Paul. They all yelled, 'What's burning, Mum?' I hadn't noticed that the room was full of greyish-blue smoke that smelled a bit like candle smoke. But I had not lit any candles for days. The smoke seemed to be coming from the newspaper rack, so Paul picked it up and took it outside into the garden. Tipping everything out, I was puzzled to find nothing wrong, but to be on the safe side I left the rack outside in the garden over night. Indoors the smoke had cleared but left a cloying smell that caught at the back of our throats. Now that the apparent danger had passed, Paul left. Within minutes small drops of water began to drip from the living room ceiling, almost like rain. Then the girls screamed from upstairs where water was also dripping from their ceiling. I had no explanation. It couldn't be a burst pipe since the water was dripping from both floors simultaneously. Eventually it stopped and we all went to bed, although the girls took some persuading. I wondered whether there was any connection between the story I had been typing and the phenomena we had experienced.

Another interesting case at this time concerned a friend's

house in the village of Harpole. Anne-Marie was a great fan of my palmistry and tarot card readings, and I had spent two memorable evenings at her house when I did readings for herself and her friends and family. She was our mobile hair-dresser, and one afternoon while cutting our hair she told me of the ghost in her house. It had frightened her and her young son. She asked me what could be done about it, and I volunteered to pop round and see what I could pick up.

She led me to the room where the haunting had taken place. It was her bedroom, and she had awoken in the semi-darkness to see the stooped figure of an old man looking at her in bed. Her son, who had crawled into bed with his parents in the middle of the night, had also seen it. The former council house is bright and modern inside and only about 40 years old. I wondered whether the apparition was a former tenant. If the ghost was of the recording type there would be little I could do, but if it was a spirit-form I might be able to talk to him and persuade him to move on. Sitting down on the bed, I started to tune in and felt the presence of a sad man. As he walked into the room the temperature dropped and I felt cold. Then I heard this old man say, 'This is my house. I didn't have a wardrobe there. That's for the dressing table. They have dug up all my vegetables. I've lost them all.' Then, after pausing briefly, he said, 'Why was there a baby in my bed?'

I told Anne-Marie all this, and she was a little shocked. At the end of the garden, now all grassed over, she had found the suggestion of a previous vegetable plot with a few shoots and tangled roots still present. She promised to restore it to its former glory. I tried to communicate with the man, telling him to go forward and leave this place in peace, for it belonged to others now. He was scaring them, and it wasn't fair. After waiting for some moments I went downstairs for a cup of tea with Anne-Marie. There has been no more trouble since. Interestingly, a neighbour who had lived nearby for many years told of an elderly man called Tom who had been a keen gardener.

Around this time our much loved dog Cheeky died after being in very poor health for several months. On several occasions while she lay on her bed in the kitchen I and the children and also one of their friends saw her shadowy form in the living room. The form was shadowy and indistinct and it shocked us, for when we looked we found Cheeky still on her bed in the kitchen. The 'dog' we had seen moved as she had done in her youth, and this *doppelganger* persisted for a couple of days. Then one morning we found her having convulsions and had to ask the vet to put her to sleep.

My feeling is that as the dog was so ill she was departing from this world little by little. The shade we saw was her consciousness wandering free of the physical body. Many legends and superstitions mention a *doppelganger* or 'double'. To see one's own double is a portent of one's death. Many people have been visited by a loved one who was many miles distant and already dead or seriously ill. I think that the departure of the spirit form from the physical body is usually sudden, but it can be more tentative and drawn-out, as in the case of our dog.

Over the last five or six years I have met many people who have experienced seeing the ghost of a beloved pet. Sceptics might argue that this is merely wishful thinking, but I think that most animal ghost sightings are recordings of actions laid down in the environment during that animal's lifetime. I do not believe that animals possess a soul such as human beings have, but there is a vital form of energy and a life-force. In Britain there are many accounts, both recent and ancient, of phantom black dogs. Often they are thought of as malevolent, but sometimes they can be protective, for example accompanying lonely travellers on their walk home. A pub in my home town boasts such a phantom, an unfriendly one whose appearance engenders fear. He is usually seen in the cellar.

II

GHOSTLY ENCOUNTERS

10

Ghost Hunts and Overnight Vigils

Overnight investigations or vigils are one of the most important aspects of ghost-hunting. The Ghost Club organize many, but the majority I have taken part in were organized by myself. These have ranged from small groups consisting of me and a friend to up to a dozen participants. Fortunately most sessions take place indoors, but sometimes outdoor locations are visited.

I find it helpful to sit in near darkness if possible. Not only does this help to concentrate the mind, but it also sets the right atmosphere. At the start of the vigil we sometimes place a small test object on a flat surface well away from the sitters with a circle drawn in chalk around it. Usually the object has some emotional significance; it may be a key, a piece of jewellery or even an old coin. Any other objects or pieces of furniture liable to move spontaneously also have a circle drawn round them to fix their exact position so that even small deviations can be detected and measured. So a stick of chalk is an important item of our kit. Thermometers are used to take frequent readings as sudden dramatic drops in room temperature are a frequent feature. Then we also need pad and pen to jot down notes and afterwards write up the proceedings. None of the equipment needs to be high tech, but there are of course researchers who use the very best in video recorders, sound equipment, geiger counters and suchlike.

One vigil of which we had high hopes took place in the churchyard at Borley in Suffolk. I went there with Dennis Moyses, a veteran ghost-hunter. Earlier on the day in question a local woman had seen what was possibly a ghost walking behind me near to where a ghostly nun is said to traverse. However, not long after we had set up our two chairs after dark a car full of yobs shouting obscenities parked their car nearby with its radio blaring, so our hopes of witnessing anything supernatural were dashed.

Any reader interested in the paranormal will need no introduction to Borley which was made famous by the ghost-hunter Harry Price. The rectory there, built in the late nineteenth century, quickly gained a reputation for being haunted. Over the years a whole catalogue of supernatural occurrences happened there, witnessed by a succession of tenant families, including the Reverend Foyster with his young bride around whom much of the activity focussed. After the rectory burnt down the activity seemed to have been transferred to the church where the above-mentioned nun walks in the cemetery and where music is said to emanate from the church late at night when it is empty. This was captured on tape by a group of investigators in the 1970s together with some inhuman groaning and sighing.

I have conducted three investigations at the World's End Pub at Ecton in Northamptonshire, and have written about two of these in detail. The third involved a challenge set by the magazine *Bizarre*, in which the reporter Mark Blacklock tells of an unusual or daring activity in which he has participated, such as running with bulls in Spain, diving from aircraft and other such feats. Spending a night in a haunted property with ghost-investigators struck me as rather tame by comparison. However, Mark seemed keen to participate in what might turn out to be a scary experience.

Dating from 1645, the World's End Pub has a long and colourful history, a perfect breeding ground for ghostly activity. The pub was named after an incident connected with the Battle of Naseby when it became a resting place for the dead and wounded soldiers after the fighting, for many of whom the cellar became literally their last stop-off in this world. It is rumoured that the pub's former garden (now a playground) became a mass burial site. Such a high saturation of suffering and death would be bound to leave its mark.

Two individual deaths are also associated with the pub, a suicide in the upstairs living quarters, and a shooting in the bar. In the flat occupied by the landlady, Belinda Blackmore, the scene of the suicide of a former landlady is in the corner of her living room where she keeps her stereo, and she was surprised when I asked whether the stereo ever malfunctioned, turning itself on, for example. She wondered how I knew, but I had only guessed, since a site where a sudden and violent death had occurred is likely to carry more negative energy, and ghosts seem to use electrical energy to manifest.

The group consisted of myself and my father, Patrick Leonard the photographer, Belinda, Mark Blacklock with a photographer from the magazine, and my son Laurie for whom this would be his first vigil. We split up into three groups, each spending approximately half-an-hour in each of the haunted rooms, the cellar, the bar and the playroom area. At the end of each stint we all met up to compare notes. The equipment we used was fairly basic: cameras, tri-field meters which pick up anomalous levels of both electrical and magnetic fields, and a tape-recorder which I left running in the dining room area, said to be haunted by a soldier, in the hope of picking up any spectral activity.

My group started in the cellar, the former war-time morgue, where we set up stools and extinguished the lights. Apart from being bombarded by an army of beer flies we did not experience much, except what seemed to be a whispered 'Welcome everybody' which no one but me heard and which may have been a misinterpretation of the drone of the ice-making machine if it was not an hallucination or a snippet of 'stone tape-recording'. Then my father, Dennis and Laurie took our place in the cellar while Belinda, the magazine photographer and my neighbour Danny took up residence in the playroom. My group settled in the bar, the scene of the shooting incident. (On our previous vigil at this spot Dennis and I had heard the distinctive sound of matches being struck one after another but had found no source of that noise.) Many customers have had spooky experiences in the bar area and in the adjacent hall where it is always extremely cold even in summer. The chill of a haunting is altogether different from normal cold.

During the first ghost investigation at the World's End Pub, two mediums, Paul and Sue Hopgood, and a young barman spent about 20 minutes in the playroom after which the barman, breathless and whitefaced, beat a hasty retreat saying that he had seen something terrible. From being utterly sceptical he had become a total believer in ghosts. In fact, he never returned to the pub although Sue and Paul were not sure what he had seen.

No such dramas occurred during the 'challenge' vigil although we did hear quite clearly some scratching sounds from inside the walls behind us which Belinda assured us could not be rats as they had regular visits from the environmental health officer. Mark Blacklock remained sceptical as is perhaps customary with journalists who have to cover so many different stories that they end up with an almost total lack of belief in anything. As happens often with vigils, nothing of significance occurred that night. Our high hopes remained unfulfilled, but this is a disappointment that ghost-hunters have to learn to live with. The article in the magazine will have reached a large audience, but it made us all sound like a cross between ghost-busters and the crew from the British *Carry on* films.

Most members of the general public have no idea what ghost-busters do or how a vigil is conducted, but I had a chance in a small way to put this right when I was invited to Charlton House at Greenwich to participate in an item on ghosts for the TV programme London Tonight. This bustling venue with its library and café and numerous rooms all used daily by various community groups, churches, schools and local musicians has plenty of ghosts. I am sure that such a high traffic of people every day helps fuel the ghostly activity, for ghosts thrive on human emotion and energy. The library used to be a chapel and its stained-glass windows generate an almost ethereal quality. It has a phantom who walks through a heavy old oak door dressed in doublet and hose, and another ghost who pinches women's bottoms if they take his fancy!

From an upstairs window visitors have seen a woman dressed in old-fashioned clothes clutching a bundle (thought to be a baby) as she scurries on her way only to vanish as suddenly and mysteriously as she appeared. The ghost of a young boy walks on one of the oak staircases. During renovation work to install a lift, the bones of a young boy were found inside one of the chimneys. It is thought that he may have become lost in the warren of chimney shafts and then fallen asleep and died. Child chimney sweeps were easily dispensed with by their Victorian masters, so he was probably forgotten and not even searched for. The legs of a phantom have been seen by numerous witnesses dangling from the ceiling in one of the upper rooms. In another room I sensed a chilling, tangible evil which others had also felt. A child had been strangled there, and as we spoke of it the producer said she felt pressure around her neck.

We decided to do the filming in a large, oak-panelled room much used for meetings and with some history of hauntings. I was to talk about how to set up a ghost watch, what equipment is used and just what to expect. We were to pretend that the filming was taking place over several hours, and at the end I had to comment on how it had all gone and then turn off the light. It felt strange to be pretending, but working on various TV shows I had already found out that television is never quite what it seems. Everything is manipulated and changed, shortened and cut down to manageable bite-sized segments. Afterwards I was sad to leave that beautiful old house with all its ghosts.

11

Video and Photographic Evidence

In response to numerous adverts placed in newspapers and *The Fortean Times* I received several photographs and videos purportedly showing ghosts, ectoplasm or UFOs. My friend the photographic expert Patrick Leonard helped me sift through them and most could be easily dismissed as having been caused by problems like 'sticky camera shutter' where any slight movement by the operator causes trails of light to register on the film in the split second's delay before the shutter functions. This explained a picture showing ecto-plasmic-like trails from wall lights. Other anomalies could be explained as simulacra, deceptive resemblances which the brain uses to construct likenesses to the human face or form in light and shade, or random patterns. Who has not done this with a knot in wood perhaps, or a stain on the wall or carpet?

A lady from Scotland sent me just such a photo from the battle site of Culloden said to depict a bonnetted Highlander. Her story of a haunting that followed her visit to Culloden was interesting, but her photo really was not. Then there was a video showing a UFO in London and strange goings on in some bushes outside a flat. The UFO clearly resembled an unleashed foil balloon being buffeted by high winds, and as for the supposed image of Jesus Christ in the bush, well, that choice of subject told me that this was probably the delusion of a schizophrenic mind.

Two gems remained, however. The video of what looked like a Quaker appearing in a Kent riding school, and a monk who appeared in a photo taken in a Buckinghamshire pub. These at least deserved a second look and offered, I felt, some degree of proof. Both locations felt right when I visited them.

The video by Martin Emmott was taken of his wife during a riding lesson at Cobham near Maidstone. She had wanted to see whether her riding looked as bad as it felt. When she watched it a few days later she was surprised to see rising up out of the ground a strangely menacing figure with a thin face and dark eyes and a shock of grey hair dressed in dark, clerical garb like that of a Quaker. Martin was at a loss to explain the extra who appeared so suddenly on his film which he therefore had checked out at a nearby film studio. The experts pronounced it to be a form that appeared spontaneously on the film and were certain that no trickery or tampering were involved. Is this very mysterious, or is it simply a face from the past, an example of 'stone tape-recording' transferred on to a video tape? Martin confirmed that he himself had seen nothing while filming. The story and footage were shown as part of the Fortean TV series on the paranormal by Channel 4.

A year later I was asked to take part in a programme being filmed at the riding stable. Having been intrigued by the video I was pleased to go. I arrived before the TV crew and had a chance to look around. I explained who I was to the owner who, it turned out, had read one of my books. He said that nothing unusual had happened recently and chuckled when I said I wanted to try and tune in psychically to see if I could

A still from the video of a Quaker ghost (see face top left) at the riding school in Cobham, Kent

find out more about his enigmatic ghost. He said he would like to test out my supposed psychic powers and I was happy to oblige. This wouldn't be the first time I was put on the spot as most people quite naturally want some proof.

Mr Broomer led me to a field and pointed to some land beyond the hedge and across a lane saying, 'Can you tell me about that field over there?' I looked across at the field and at first got nothing. Then I let my mind wander and just spoke the first words that entered my mind: 'That field – everyone died. It was a village – the plague – horrible.' The words tumbled out, and when no more came I glanced at Mr Broo-

mer for his response. His face was a picture of astonishment.
'You're right, but how could you have known?' He told me that
in medieval times there had been a small village where the
field now was. The population had been entirely wiped out by
the plague; there hadn't even been anyone left to bury the
dead. Eventually the dwellings were knocked down and covered with soil and the area grassed over. Even now it could
only be used for grazing and not ploughed because bones and
rubble from the past might be uncovered. I wondered whether
this sorry tale might contain clues to the ghost that appeared
so dramatically in the video. Was that man one of the unfor-
tunates who had perished there?

The film crew asked me to walk around the riding school's
ménage and talk to camera about anything I picked up. It was
a sea of mud after a period of heavy rain, and I sighed about
my lovely new black suede boots. Having walked around for a
while I suddenly came upon an area of distinct unpleasant-
ness, a zone of only a couple of square feet. I stood there
quietly and focussed, remembering Martin's video and its
apparition. Facts came flooding in, and with the cameras
rolling I spoke of the impressions I was picking up. A man had
died on this spot long ago, and he had a connection with the
plague village. Although he had been a religious man, he had
lost his faith shortly before his untimely death and openly
cursed his god. His bones lay underneath my feet. I remember
a cold sensation and my body shaking. I asked the film crew
whether they could fetch a spade so that I might dig for bones.
But understandably Mr Broomer would have none of it. He
was planning to build a stable block there and promised to let
me know if any remains were uncovered in the process. I went

home emotionally drained and feeling a great deal of sympathy for the lost soul I had connected with.

The next piece of evidence concerns the photo sent by Mrs Pat Sharpe taken in the bar area of the Kings Arms pub at Newport Pagnell in Buckinghamshire. A local photographer had taken it over a decade ago, and I hoped and believed that it was genuine. He had shot only one roll of film and while he did so the landlord's dog went berserk and had to be shut outside. Neither man saw or sensed anything unusual. When the photographer developed his film he was dismayed to find that seven shots appeared to be spoiled with what first looked like smudging in the right-hand corner. Soon he realized that these were not smudges but the semi-transparent figure of a monk. In each shot he had moved slightly. The image was quite clear. The hooded figure has a rope round his waist and holds what looks like a cane in his extended hand. His habit is a dull brown colour. The pub stands in the grounds of what was once Tickford Abbey.

The landlord knew that the premises were haunted as customers and staff had felt, heard and seen various things over the years. One of the pictures was printed in the local paper and the photographer was offered a large amount of money by a national newspaper, but he refused to sell, for he was not interested in making money out of it. When I first saw the photograph it struck me as a case of 'stone tape-recording'. The monk who had presumably been a member of the long-gone abbey community is semi-transparent as though faded with time to such an extent that the two people present that day failed to notice him even though the Alsatian dog did. Most of the photos of ghosts that hold up under scrutiny have

The ghostly monk photographed at the Kings Arms pub, Newport Pagnell

in common that the person taking them did not notice the ghostly extra at the time.

The last category of photographic phantoms, my favourite really, are the Cinderella of ghost photography, often over-looked, but in fact worthy of study. These are the blobs of light, orbs or fog-like shapes seen beside a person. My sister had just such a photo of her baby daughter looking straight at a fog near her. It was taken when they lived in an old cottage in the village of Wallgrave. This is the most common type of spirit photography. Of course there are often other explanations for such blobs, and unfortunately it is easy to fake pictures using photography. Nevertheless, I am sure that many such pictures taken in houses that are haunted or have noticeable cold spots are genuine.

12

Woodford Church – the Disembodied Heart

Woodford is a small village near Kettering in Northamptonshire. Many decades ago workers renovating the church there found a heart which is now placed in a small bamboo box behind a glass screen in one of the pillars halfway down the church. It is the heart of Walter Trayli, a crusader. In the days when he was killed, only the heart was brought home for burial because the rest of the body would decompose during the long journey.

In an interview on the local radio I happened to hear John Hawes, a wine expert, mention a séance he had participated in 30 years ago which concerned a ghost in Woodford church. I rang to ask whether I could interview him about this for one of my books, and we agreed to meet in the church where he could show me the place where the heart had been interred. It was a stormy afternoon, so I waited in my car until John arrived. We ran through the rain to the heavy oak door which he unlocked with a large iron key.

The séance John now told me about had taken place in the White Horse Pub at Lowick together with two spiritualists and another friend. They constructed an ouija board to which they put all the usual questions, such as, 'Is there anybody there?' Then they asked a question to which none of them knew the answer. 'What is the name of the person whose heart is interred in the walls of Woodford church?' Rapidly a reply was spelled out: 'T R A' and then the glass shot from the table, smashing against the wall. John had been scared and left in a hurry on his motorbike. Next day the vicar told him that the heart was thought to belong to Sir Walter Trayli, the first three letters of whose name the ouija board had spelt out. John was thoroughly shocked.

At about the time of John's séance a schoolboy had taken a number of photographs in the church for a school project. One of these showed a figure kneeling at the altar seemingly at prayer. This photo has since been featured in many books, and it is also pinned up on the church notice board for all to see. John wondered whether his séance had made the Trayli spirit restless.

As we sat in the church we heard thunder rolling overhead and sensed the electric atmosphere of a storm in the air. I asked John some more questions about that night over 30 years ago and he admitted that those events still scared him. Having been one who scoffed at the supernatural he had become a firm believer, but had sworn never to 'dabble' again. I heard a scuffling sound coming from the front of the church and John was aghast when I asked whether there was anyone else in the building. He pointed out that we had let ourselves in with a key. I went to see whether there were any mice, and as I opened the small iron gate leading to the front part of the building I asked the perennial question, 'Is there anyone there?' In reply came the tinkling sound of a small handbell. I asked the question again, whereupon I was literally pushed to one side by a tall, cloaked figure that looked stretched and

The parish church of Woodford, Northampton

elongated and was totally transparent, like a piece of black-and-white cine film. Simultaneously I was swamped by a musty, unpleasant smell. John sat transfixed, ashen grey and with a look of absolute terror on his face.

The apparition had gone, and I went and sat down beside John. I asked whether he was alright, but the look of him bothered me and I feared he might die there and then. I asked him to describe what he had seen and he simply replied that it had been the ghost of Sir Walter Trayli. Glancing beyond him, I then saw the figure sitting there right beside him. He turned towards it and in an instant leapt from his seat and ran from the church, slamming the door behind him. The ghost had gone, perhaps scared by all the noise and commotion. Finding John outside I said we should go back in to find out whether whoever it was wanted to communicate a message. John said I could go if I wanted to. He thought I was insane and he wished he had never met me. I did go back in, but the atmosphere had totally changed, and I noticed that the storm had also abated. Could there be a connection?

We made our way back to John's cottage where he invited me in. His wife was quite shocked by his appearance, and if she had not seen him 'looking as though he'd seen a ghost' would scarcely have believed what we told her. After making tea for us she fetched an old book chronicling the history of Woodford and its church. Among many other things it mentioned a small brass handbell that had been rung before special services but had long since disappeared, perhaps stolen.

I told a friend from the Ghost Club about this adventure, and he asked me to write it up for the club magazine. He also suggested we try and arrange an overnight vigil at the church, and I was very keen to do this. I rang the vicar who was quite angry and practically accused me of conjuring up the ghost. She did not believe in the paranormal and would not agree to a vigil. Her vehemence called to mind Shakespeare's words 'the lady doth protest too much', but I did not want to press our request as I had no wish to upset her.

Many months later John rang to ask whether I would join him on BBC Radio Northampton to talk about our experience. I was delighted to find him perfectly recovered. The programme went well and the message we wanted to get across to our audience was that our experience was true, for it is totally unlikely that we could both have hallucinated the same thing. I have since heard that after our sighting the Woodford ghost has been very active with many reported incidents both visual and auditory.

13

The Ghost at the Newsagents'

To make ends meet I decided to get a job in a local shop and work shifts around the children and also have time for my writing and, most importantly, investigations. The shop is in Towcester and overlooks the old market square which is now a car park. Watling Street, the old Roman road, cuts right through the town. Many of the houses in the street are several hundred years old and give it an air of quaintness.

On my first day I had to do a training programme on the computer which required considerable concentration as I am somewhat computer-illiterate. The computer was in a corner of the back warehouse which was crammed to overflowing with Christmas stock. After about an hour I sensed someone looking at me and turned round, thinking it might be the manager checking up on my progress. But there was no one there, so I turned back to the screen. Almost immediately I heard a voice, 'Hello, I'm Harry, this shop, all this used to belong to me, but now I'm dead.' I spun round thinking one of the staff was playing a trick on me, but again no one was there, and I noticed that the room had turned icy cold so that my breath was coming out as vapour. I was unsure what to do, since this was my first day at work there and I didn't know any of the other staff. Then the voice spoke again, this time telling me that his throat hurt and that he had died upstairs.

I went to the office to ask the manager whether the shop was haunted and she asked, 'Who told you?' I said that the ghost 'Harry' had told me of his death upstairs and that his throat hurt. She was astonished that the spirit had spoken to me and confirmed that he was often active around the warehouse. He had owned the shop and rumour had it that he had hung himself in one of the upstairs rooms in a fit of depression. Her mother had lived locally for over 60 years, and she would be bound to know what his name had been.

The next day she confirmed that the name was Harry. The workers and both the managers were quite surprised at all the information I had picked up but everyone believed me for they were used to the strange goings-on in the shop. Stock would be found moved about in the warehouse after it had been locked up for the night. There were also cold spots in the shop and sometimes things like bread would fall to the floor as if pushed by an invisible hand. A shadowy form is also seen quite regularly walking along the liquor aisle. He is always seen from the corner of your eye, and when you turn thinking it is a customer you find that the shop is empty. I found that within a few days this was happening quite frequently, sometimes more than once in a single shift. Each time he seemed to catch me out.

Other things also happened. Quite often cigarettes were thrown at the cashiers from the dispenser behind them. On one occasion I felt a sharp pain on my ankle and when I looked down I noticed a small red indentation where I had felt the impact. On the floor beside my foot was a pound coin, the missile that had hit me. There was no one in the shop. The thrower would have had to crouch low and throw the coin with considerable force. On closing my till at the end of the shift, I found I was exactly one pound up.

As I work two early shifts I usually see the milkman and whoever is there makes him a cup of tea. Once he was rather shocked to hear us discussing the ghost and although he made light of it, thereafter we noticed a distinct change in his behaviour. He no longer wanted to go to the back warehouse alone and took to bringing someone else with him. We teased him mercilessly. One day the younger fellow he brought with him had an encounter with Harry who told him most severely, 'Go away, I don't like you.' This only fuelled the milkman's fears. My most recent encounter was a pleasant one. I was working on the computer when I heard a whispered 'I love you'. There was no one there except a customer at the far end of the shop. I was sure I wasn't mistaken for I felt the familiar tingly vibration you get when someone leans close and whispers directly into your ear.

I think that Harry has yet to move on. He has been a steady presence in the place for many years and I hope he will remain for many more to come. He does not frighten or bother the staff but remains a sort of benign and watchful presence in the shop he once knew as his own.

14

Pengersick Castle

A television company asked me and several other members of the Ghost Club to join in filming an overnight investigation at Pengersick Castle near Penzance in Cornwall. It was to be part of a programme called 'Haunted England' and would also feature other sights with a strong reputation for paranormal activity. I was not in good shape, having not quite recovered from a bout of flu, and because of terrible weather Dennis Moyses and I could only get as far as Bristol by train and had to continue our journey in a hired car. We were both very weary when we arrived and were introduced to the members of the film crew. There were several other members of the Ghost Club and four students from Bristol as novices in the proceedings. Filming was to take place overnight, but local bed-and-breakfast beds were booked for a few hours sleep when it ended. The film crew took us all for a pub meal to fortify us for the night's work ahead. This was my first visit to Cornwall, and over cider and delicious food I became excited about what might lie ahead. Little did I know that it was to be a night that almost put me off ghost-hunting for good.

The castle looked beautiful from the outside despite the grim, driving rain and cold wind. Its size surprised me, for it was more like a small tower. In the past I have always felt a strong affinity with castles, even longing to live in one when I was a child. The thickness of the walls and solid feeling of a building that had stood firm for centuries fired my imagination, as did the thought of living alongside the colourful characters of the past.

But this castle was not attractive, and the first thing I noticed as we entered was the unmistakable odour of cats' urine. The place was in a shocking state, very dirty and unkempt with cats wandering all over the place. For centuries the ancestral seat of the Godolphin family, its history was peppered with witchcraft, murder and ghosts. My colleague Robert Snow, who has a long connection with it, claims it is one of the most haunted buildings in the British Isles.

The film crew took several hours setting up atmospheric lighting and generally getting ready to film, and to cap it all the place was freezing. Despite the cups of tea they made us we felt we had been kept waiting for far too long, and being in the final stages of flu I felt rotten.

Realizing we were in for a long night I decided to sneak off to tune in on my own and try to discover why I had such a strong initial dislike of the place. Climbing the narrow spiral stone staircase I found the bedchamber which was the most actively haunted room in the castle. Compared with the rest of the building it was quite nicely kept. The big bed with its faded tapestry covers was in the centre and there was a small fireplace, a chair, a mirror and a chest of drawers. Perhaps the layout of the furniture had remained unchanged for a long time.

Sitting down in the chair with my hands in my lap I breathed out. I sat quietly losing myself in thought and trying to let my mind empty itself of all distractions. After some minutes a feeling of sadness swept over me and a picture flooded into my mind in full colour. I could even smell wood burning and the wax of the candle. A woman giving birth was lying on the bed writhing in agony with hands and legs tied to the bedposts. She was attended by a woman dressed in a long gown with her hair tied up and her face wet with sweat. Somehow I knew they were mother and daughter. The baby was born quickly but had no chance to utter a cry before the attending woman reached for a knife and killed it, stabbing it repeatedly uttering vile curses as she did so. Then she wrapped it in a rag and threw it on to the fire. There was a sense of terrible evil in that small bedroom. I felt sick and opened my eyes. I knew that I had not imagined what I had seen and the horror showed on my face as I looked at myself in the mirror which was misty and grey at the edges. I wondered whether the murderess had looked in the same mirror.

Returning downstairs I reported on what I had seen. Robert Snow told me that some years earlier another member of the Ghost Club had experienced more or less the identical vision. Robert knew that both infanticide and witchcraft had taken place in the castle and said that the woman who had killed that poor child had probably been a witch. Meanwhile the film crew were still not ready and brushed aside our requests to hurry up a bit. We were all fed up with waiting and I felt cold and shivery with flu. To cap it all, when filming finally started I sat down in a pool of cat's wee.

Robert made a good job of hosting the programme, intro-ducing us all and speaking of what a vigil involved. Then we all tramped up to a room on the floor above where it was warmer and more pleasant. We turned out most of the lights and I began speaking to the spirits of that place. I asked them to make their presence known to us either by manifestation or by moving one of the test objects Robert had placed on the table. Almost immediately the temperature of the room dropped and when we switched on the light we saw that it had gone down by some 10 degrees. Then one of the students cried out that she had seen the face of a woman with long hair at the window and I wondered out loud whether it was the witch. But the girl, somewhat shaken, asked me not to talk about it. Nothing more happened as we waited for another 40 minutes, so the producer asked us to move up to the bed-chamber on the next floor.

We were all flagging by now, having been up for what felt like days. I repeated my pleas to the spirits in the room to come and communicate, but the room remained quiet. After about an hour we decided to finish, and I joked with Phillip that with all the messing about at the beginning perhaps even the ghosts had got fed up and left. The producer then asked us all on camera what we had thought of the evening and our view of the castle. Not surprisingly most of the comments were lukewarm. One of the students said the evening had been interesting but had not bolstered his belief in ghosts. Robert still felt the castle to be the most haunted in England but we had been unlucky. When it came to my turn I didn't mince my words, saying quite rudely that this had been one of the worst nights of my life and that the place was depressing and infused with evil. It was still raining as we drove to our beds. I had never been so glad to leave a place. By contrast our quarters were cosy and modern. Quietly letting myself in, I crept up to my room, threw my disgustingly filthy clothes on the floor, had a bit of a wash and climbed into a blissfully clean bed. It was 6 a.m. and I had been awake for more than 24 hours.

But sleep did not come yet. I felt a horrible presence enter the room even though the door remained firmly shut. I recognized it immediately as the witch from the castle who had followed me back. (This had only happened to me once before when I interviewed a man about a poltergeist in his home. Whatever it was followed me back and smashed up my young son's guitar in the night.) I asked the woman to leave me alone as I needed to sleep and would pay no attention to her. As I curled up into a ball I felt her standing by the bed looking at me with great interest. Having decided never again to take part in such events I finally fell into a deep sleep of utter exhaustion.

I awoke at noon with the sun shining through the curtains. Having forced myself to put on my filthy clothes I walked to the dining room where one of the students was tucking in to a hearty breakfast. I piled my plate with the good fare our kind hostess had cooked for us, and drank several cups of tea. The producer and his assistant tried to persuade us to stay for another night's filming but Dennis, Phillip and I had all had enough. Grudgingly they gave us our travel expenses and we set off for home. I believe Robert was disappointed with us as he loves the castle, but I felt too filthy and was longing to see my children. It was the kind of misery that arises when you have looked forward to something only to find the experience bitterly disappointing and horrible.

Once home, my doubts about future vigils dissipated, of

course, but I had learnt a valuable lesson. Never set off for a ghost vigil without a set of clean clothes, always take a bottle of water, and allow for at least 12 hours when a film crew assure you that something will only take six!

15

The House at Peterborough

Dennis Moyses called to tell me about a house which a very active ghost was making uninhabitable. The girlfriend of the owner, whom I shall call 'Dave', was refusing to spend even one night there, and if the matter could not be resolved the house would have to be sold. I am usually loathe to attempt to move ghosts on as to me many of them are a small bit of our history and heritage, and I feel we should love them and preserve them. But I am happy to help when a situation becomes untenable, so I agreed to do my best for 'Dave' but sent a message saying I could not promise that I would be successful.

Another member of the Ghost Club and a local medium were to join Dennis and me, and we all set off for what turned out to be a very ordinary looking, bay-fronted Victorian terraced house set back slightly from the road. 'Dave' and his girlfriend were very friendly and grateful to us for our interest. I began by asking them what they had seen and heard and who else had experienced anything. While 'Dave' did not mind the phenomena, 'Deborah' felt she could not live with the haunting. She seemed a quiet, introverted woman, and I wondered why she should feel traumatized to the extent of being unable to live in a haunted house. The couple left us, and we began by wandering around separately, taking our time, as work on the psychic level should never be rushed. The house was in some disarray as it was being extensively refurbished. There were paint pots in corners, rolls of carpet waiting to be laid, and pictures stacked against walls.

I felt no atmosphere in the lounge or kitchen but definitely sensed something in the hall. It is most usual for a bedroom and staircase to be haunted, and in this case I felt the activity to be concentrated in the back bedroom and landing area. In the box room Dennis found a cupboard. Scored deep into the wood were the words, 'Relationships get ill, bullets kill', and some other doodles as well. There was also a pile of exercise books with similar phrases, perhaps written down by a teenager suffering some kind of torment.

When we were ready to begin we gathered chairs and arranged them in a circle. Everyone agreed that the only active rooms were this bedroom and the landing, and we all sensed a male presence. With the curtains drawn we sat in the semi-darkness holding hands and quietly trying to tune in to whoever was haunting the house. One of us said a prayer. After a long time I heard a young male voice almost whisper, 'Hello, my name is Frank'. I replied aloud, 'Hello Frank, my name is Natalie. We are here to help you, but for us to do that you will need to help us. Frank, why are you haunting this place? You are scaring the good people who want to live here now.' After a while he spoke more loudly and sounded angry. 'This is my house. I can't leave. This is my bedroom. I was hurt in the war — my leg. They sent me home with all this metal in my legs. I stayed in bed waiting for them to heal. They never did. Gangrene set in. Do you know what gangrene smells like?

Nobody could stand to be in the same room as me, not even my mother.'

I related all this to the others and then asked Frank about his mother as I sensed there had been problems between them. I asked whether he ever went on to the landing. (An electrician working late one night in the empty house had seen a man at the top of the stairs. Scared, he had downed tools and fled, never to return.) 'Of course I go to the top of the stairs and bang on the wall to call mother.' We gradually built up a picture of a man in torment, cut off in his prime, slowly festering to death in his bed feeling abandoned and unloved. He told us to look at the pictures behind us on the floor, saying that one of them looked like his mother and he didn't like it. We found a photo of a tall, chic woman smoking a cigarette. It was the one Frank meant.

Frank wanted his room painted green like it used to be. I asked him to forgive those who had hurt him and let go of his anger and resentment, for this would free him to move on to the next stage. He seemed reluctant at first but promised he would try. We all sat for some time thinking about the story that had unfolded.

I sensed a dramatic change in the atmosphere of the room, a lifting of the oppression. Although it was now much later in the day and the curtains were still closed the room seemed lighter. The others also sensed a change, and Dennis now told us that another medium had visited before us and had also picked up on a Frank who had died during the war. I felt we had achieved what we set out to do and realized just how exhausted I was feeling. This kind of work very quickly saps one's energy.

Driving home I found it hard to get poor Frank out of my mind, thinking of the horrible way his life had ended. Next day 'Dave' phoned to thank me but said that 'Deborah' still felt nervous and he wondered how he could reassure her. I suggested he might help her gradually to spend more and more time in the house until she felt comfortable there. I also hinted that he might like to paint the bedroom green and get rid of the picture Frank didn't like, adding that if he had any more problems he should ring me again. As yet I have heard nothing, so I hope that no news is good news. It is very sad when a ghost drives people in fear from their home and I will always try to help and comfort those concerned.

16

Memorable Cases

A Portent of Evil

Whilst I was busy researching material for my last book *The Ghost Hunting Casebook* I visited a woman named Pat Sharp to enquire about a possible ghost in Salcey forest. Almost as an aside, however, she told me of an incident which was far more interesting but also chilling in the extreme. She may even have told me about it so that it would be documented in the hope that, should the horrifying incident come to pass, she would be believed. Her husband found it all difficult to credit.

Pat told me that about 12 years earlier she had settled down with a cup of coffee for a quiet read of the local paper. What she saw on the front page was a most upsetting story about a father who had killed his wife and three children and then himself. The murders had occurred in a cottage on the edge of Salcey forest. Pat knew the isolated cottages well from taking her dogs for walks in the vicinity. She was extremely shocked and so, according to the article, were the police. Here was an apparently motiveless crime in which the perpetrator had died along with his victims. Still upset, Pat put down the paper and busied herself making her husband's tea.

After tea, Pat remembered the story and told her husband

about it, and then went to fetch the paper to show him. She found it on the floor and took it to him. He turned all the pages and then, puzzled, remarked that she must have been mistaken, for there was no murder story on the front page or on any other page. He was right, the front page was totally different and altogether more pleasant. Pat could not understand it and wondered whether she had dreamt it all, yet it had seemed so real.

Next day, still disturbed, she rang the local newspaper who told here they had never heard of such a story, and she had a similar reply from the police when she rang them next. In fact, Pat was so upset by her 'vision' that a few days later she even visited the cottage in question where she was met by a very baffled owner who thought her a bit mad. Gradually she tried to forget the whole experience.

There was an edge of certainty and conviction in her voice as she told me all this, but it was also tinged with sadness. 'I just know those murders are going to happen,' she said. 'I do believe that I somehow saw the future that day.'

Strange to say, such stories have been reported before. People have seen 'phantom' reports of events in newspapers, on television, even on Ceefax and computers. Sometimes the events foretold have come to pass and sometimes not, or else the 'vision' referred to something much further into the future. Sometimes, perhaps, such witnesses are mistaken, or have dreamt such things. Yet there are even reports of more than one witness seeing the material portrayed in this way at the same time. This raises important questions as to the way we understand time, the media and the very malleable stuff of which our own present and future are made.

The Woman's Strange Smile

Jean, who does not consider herself to be psychic, since she has never had a similar experience either before or since, told me what had happened while she and her husband had been on holiday on the Isle of Wight. She had a terrible nightmare during their first night there. She saw a large house. In one of the rooms a young woman in Victorian dress was having an argument with her brother, also quite young. The woman stepped on to a small balcony at the front of the house and, as her brother followed her, more heated words were exchanged until the young man pushed his sister in his anger. She fell with a cry on to the paved terrace below. She hit her head but did not die instantly. As she lay in a pool of blood she had a beatific smile on her face.

Jean woke up screaming and it took her husband a long time to calm her down. She felt she had witnessed a real event. The weather was so bad next morning that the couple decided to visit an indoor attraction instead of exploring the island, and set off for a stately home nearby. After a very interesting tour of the house Jean asked the guide whether the place had any resident ghosts. The guide proceeded to tell her the story of a woman quarrelling with her brother and falling off the balcony. She had not died immediately, so there had been time for the local priest to administer the last rites, after which she passed away with a smile of peace on her lips. Although she did not need to go, Jean went out into the rain to look at the outside of the house, which was exactly as she had seen it in her dream. Her husband was shocked to realize that his wife had related the dream to him only hours before.

Having been very upset by the whole experience, Jean went to see her local vicar on returning home. He told her not to worry, and prayed for her, asking her to pray also for the peace of the woman who had fallen to her death.

Still traumatized when she met me, Jean wondered why the incident had been portrayed to her and not her husband, for example. I told her that when we are in a dream state our mind is much more receptive and open to our environment, as well as to the past and the future. The event had been highly emotional with the heated argument, the woman's fall and her pain, presumably her brother's regret and sadness, and finally the priest's haste to reach her before it was too late.

On many occasions I have visited places of great tragedy and become swept up in the residual emotion of the place. This happened once on Cyprus at the scene of a massacre after the Turkish invasion. I had been overcome with a feeling of hopelessness and depression and couldn't wait to leave the place. I felt that Jean had similarly felt the emotions from the past, which are available to a receptive person such as she is. Nevertheless, the accuracy and detail of her dream were exceptional, right down to the expression on the dead woman's face, which was so at odds with what one would have expected.

Memories of India

My friend Pat told me of two strange things that had happened to her in India where she had lived for many years, growing to love that beautiful country.

While living there she discovered by accident that she had the unusual talent of being able to predict earthquakes with considerable accuracy. A bad migraine she suffered one day was followed the next day by an earthquake in a neighbouring district. She mentioned this to a neighbour whom she saw almost daily and who told her that earthquakes happen nearly every month somewhere in India. Pat bet she would foresee the next one, and didn't have to wait long. Having had a migraine one day and predicting an earthquake, she read in the newspaper next day that there had been one in a district too far away for her or her neighbour to have felt anything. After this the matter became something of a joke between the two friends, but soon Pat's gift was to save their lives. She felt a sense of dread and persuaded her friend to leave the building with her. As they did so, a severe earthquake struck the district. Their apartment block was badly damaged, with the furniture and possessions inside being thrown all over the place. Had the women remained inside they may not have escaped injury or even death.

The next strange thing involved the same friend and her husband. The husband had had a disturbing 'dream' in which a ghostly monk had stood at the foot of his bed. He woke up shaken and trembling, convinced that the monk had come to fetch him, meaning that he was going to die. He was quite young, and his wife told him to pull himself together. As the wife told this to Pat, both women laughed at the husband's seemingly irrational logic. A few days later the friend's husband rang Pat and was so distraught that it took a while for her to understand and digest what he was telling her. Her good friend and neighbour, who had been chatting with her only the day before, had died suddenly.

The husband had been right about the monk's mission but wrong about the person to whom it referred.

The Woman in Pinny and Slippers

Cases that provide verification and some measure of proof are important to the ardent ghost-hunter and researcher. Not only do they provide a sense of satisfaction when all the loose ends can be tied up, but they are also more convincing to the reader since there are fewer unanswered questions. Even when some of the mechanics of a haunting remain elusive, proof of any sort is a wonderful thing.

In 1998 a case like this almost fell into my lap. My sister Kate had recently moved into a 1950s terraced house which had previously been occupied by an elderly couple who had changed very little in it and left a good deal of furniture there after the old lady died and the husband moved into a nursing home. We all helped Kate with her redecorating and I teased her that I felt Mrs Scarlet hadn't left the house. Along with her belongings she seemed to me to be still in residence in some small way. My sister forgot my remarks, which was fortunate as she has always been slightly afraid of ghosts and spirits.

It was a few weeks later when I received an excited phone call from her. Dave her boyfriend had been watching TV in the lounge when he saw a ghost, an elderly woman with grey hair and dressed in a pinny, shuffling along the hallway in her slippered feet. Being engrossed in the programme, Kate had seen nothing.

Dave had looked very shocked. (Kate had told him nothing about the previous history of the house or my earlier remarks.) At first she had disbelieved him, but he had refused to back down, so she phoned me for advice. She wanted me to talk to him, thinking that the prospect of his story being written up might make the truth come out. So I went over to interview him the next evening. While assuring me that of course he didn't 'believe in ghosts and all that nonsense' he told me about the old woman he had seen in the hallway.

The story was interesting, so I wrote up my notes and filed them away. A short while later Live TV contacted me, wanting to cover one of my ghost cases. The incident in Kate's house sprang to mind because it was so recent. Dave agreed to be interviewed on camera, so in due course the crew arrived and set up their equipment. The researcher interviewed Dave and Kate and re-enacted the brief sighting. Then she spoke to some of the neighbours and asked for a description of the late Mrs Scarlet. One long-term friend of the deceased was full of information, describing her as being short and neat with tidy grey hair. She was rarely seen without her pinny and slippers. This was word for a word a description of Dave's reported ghost even down to her particular form of shuffling gait. It was all rather impressive.

The next day the researcher rang in some embarrassment to tell me that on doing the usual checks at the studio the team had found that while they had all the pictures they had no sound whatsoever although they had checked on this repeatedly during the day's work. So they had to return the following week to re-shoot the whole programme. I believe that the anomaly in the sound recording might have been an example of a strong electro-magnetic field that not only caused Dave's initial sighting but also had the 'power' to wipe the audio tapes. Or the ghost, if she was not of the more common recording type, had the ability to drain available energies be they electrical or physical. Actually, Kate's hallway, the location of the ghost's appearance, often feels cold (despite new central heating) which is a common indication of ghostly activity.

Margaret's Return

From my years of research into so-called 'crisis apparitions' I have come to the conclusion that it is actually quite common for the bereaved to see their loved one's ghost after death. This usually happens in the two weeks after the death. The following case is a good example.

Ian contacted me after hearing a radio broadcast I did for the BBC in 1999. First he related a short incident of a haunting in his home when he was six years old. Then he told me about his experiences following the death of his wife from motor neurone disease. Ian had nursed her at home for three years, but eventually she had to be cared for in hospital where she died aged 64. Margaret, he said, had been a firm believer in an afterlife and had always promised that if she went first she would find a way to come back and offer proof (a common enough statement, actually). Ian, however, did not believe in such things and in his logical way dismissed his wife's remarks until some years later when events caused him to reconsider his opinions.

The night after Margaret's death he had a vivid dream in which he spent many hours with his wife firstly in a bungalow (scene of a previous holiday) and then enjoying a meal at a favourite restaurant. At the end of the dream she left him at the bungalow, saying she had to go. Ian is sure he saw the silhouette of her father waiting outside the door. This dream amazed him, for it was real and vivid and utterly unlike any previous ones. Nevertheless, he dismissed it as part of the grieving process for he was, after all, very sad and depressed at the time.

Following this, Ian twice saw a woman near his home who, he was sure, could have been Margaret. Glancing out of an upstairs window in the winter, he saw a woman standing in the field outside. She was wearing a yellow summer dress with a stole around her shoulders. With her was a dog that looked like their old dog Bobby. She was quite a distance away but appeared to be looking at the house.

On the next occasion Ian saw a woman like Margaret as it was getting dark. She was standing under a street lamp and was thus clearly visible. He was puzzled as to why she was wearing summer clothes in winter. He half-believed it must be Margaret, and indeed he had a photograph of her wearing those very clothes on holiday when she had been in her fifties and in good health.

Then came a further incident which pushed Ian into questioning his beliefs entirely, as he now began to believe that his wife had indeed returned in some way to offer proof and a degree of comfort. After sorting through his wife's things he was resting and sad on the day in question. As he dozed he felt someone sit down on the other end of the sofa. Half opening his eyes he saw his wife who leaned forward and pressed her hand lightly against his cheek. This woke Ian up fully with a start. Margaret was gone, but her husband could distinctly feel the pressure of her fingers on his face.

As Ian related these experiences to me his voice was choked with emotion. It was obvious that he was still coming to terms with his wife's death. His logical mind was telling him that what had transpired could not be possible, but his heart was saying something entirely different.

I find it significant that Ian saw his late wife as she had been a decade earlier when she was happy and healthy. It is easy for a sceptic to dismiss such stories, saying that grief and longing for the loved one could trigger visual and auditory halluci-nations. Perhaps this does happen in some cases, but the fact that such incidents are so commonly reported, in all cultures and by researchers from all over the world, leads me to con-clude that there must be some truth in this phenomenon. These incidents deserve much further investigation and also our respect.

The Mystery Woman with the Umbrella

There are places in the British Isles which have acquired a reputation for incidents of paranormal activity. These are referred to as 'window areas' or 'hotspots'. One of these is at Borley in Suffolk. Although the infamous rectory no longer stands, the church has many legends of ghostly activity asso-ciated with the building itself and the grounds it stands in. I had written about it briefly in my book *The Ghost Hunting*

Casebook but had never actually visited the site. I did so in 1998 together with Dennis Moyses who warned me that the local people were very fed up with the hordes of ghost-hunters who regularly descend on their village even though very little paranormal activity has in fact happened for quite some time.

We arrived there in the afternoon and decided to visit the church on the pretext of being stained-glass enthusiasts compiling a book. The village was small and quaint and strikingly tranquil. The churchyard is green and pretty, dotted with well-trimmed topiary trees and hedges. On entering the church we were surprised to be greeted by two friendly ladies dispensing tea. Apparently on that day churches around the country were offering refreshments to cyclists on sponsored runs in aid of church funds. The ladies offered us tea and then kindly gave us a tour around the church. Soon we were so engrossed that we didn't notice the departure of some cyclists who had also been looking round. One thing the ladies showed us was a pane of glass broken by vandals who had entered the church at night and stolen the collection box and chalice.

Suddenly one of them rushed to the door saying she had seen a woman carrying an umbrella pass by. But when she looked out seconds later the woman had vanished. I had been standing with my back to the door and thus been facing the wrong way so, ironically, the two eager ghost-hunters had seen nothing while the reluctant local had, in all probability, seen a ghost.

We left, determined to return after dark. By 10.30 p.m. the evening was very cold as we parked our car some distance away and then set up our folding chairs in the churchyard hoping to sit quietly and see the ghostly nun who is said to walk the grounds at night. What happened surprised us both and led us to understand the attitude of the local people. A car full of noisy individuals arrived. They parked in front of the church and proceeded to make an infernal din shouting loudly and with their car radio turned on full blast. From what they were saying it was obvious that they, too, were making an attempt at ghost-hunting. But we knew that it would be pointless to carry on our investigation with all that noise going on, so we packed up our things and left full of sympathy for the villagers whom we had previously thought of as spoil-sports.

Psychic Impressions at Lesnes Abbey

I visited Lesnes Abbey with a journalist, a medium and my photographer friend Patrick Leonard. A colourful legend attaches to the abbey about a bloody fight in which one of the monks was decapitated. The murderer was duly executed and buried beneath the main archway where he would be forever walked upon. The ghost of a headless monk is much reported on and seen regularly.

We decided to begin by walking around the grounds separately, and I set off with my field meter to see whether it would detect any strong electrical or magnetic fields in or around the ruins. If present, these would indicate good conditions for a recording-type ghost. However, I found very little evidence of any haunting, but did pick up an impression of a past connection with herbalism and healing. I believed that the monks had been actively engaged in growing herbs and studying their use in aiding the healing of the human body.

We then went to the tourist information office close by to find out more of the history of the place which had been founded in the thirteenth century by Richard de Luci and dissolved by Henry VIII. The monks had worn black habits, and a journal kept by a monk named William documented the growing of herbs and plants for medicinal purposes. This information bore out my psychic impressions and gave me a small shiver of excitement.

A park attendant assisted us with some further background, adding that there were many reports of ghostly activity connected with the ruins. He also said that the site attracted witches who used the ruins for their mysterious rituals, usually

Photo: Patrick Leonard

The ruins of Lesnes Abbey, London

under cover of darkness. He told us that he had once been frightened by coming on a young woman dressed in robes. She had spun round singing and chanting, and from the trees a large group of resident crows had taken flight and circled above her as if mesmerized. He had left in alarm, not wanting any contact with the young witch.

During the day the site is often overrun by small children noisily clambering over the chalky, grey stones, glad to escape the confines of nearby London. There is a clever example of a simulacrum that can be viewed from a certain spot. If you look long enough (and it helps if you squint), the stonework beyond a small archway, bathed in shadow, remarkably resembles a monk with his head bent forward looking at an open book in his hand.

As far as I was concerned the day was not a total waste of time even though we found little evidence of ghostly activity. Many expect such a place to be haunted, but it is not always the case at all. Perhaps expectation coupled with imagination played their part at this site. But the fact that I had quite easily picked up a sense of past activities showed that some tangible traces have remained in the fabric of the buildings. I do feel that all human action, thought and feeling holds the 'potential' for imprinting on the surroundings a trace of its former existence.

Raining down Stones

Debbie was working for her cousin as a live-in groom on the small estate of Northcoate Manor which had once been an inn on the old overnight coaching route from London to Penzance but was now a spacious family home. One of the fields next to a stream at the rear of the house had always been surrounded by speculation, and the deeds of the Manor stipulated that it was to be left untouched. It had thus been left fallow and unploughed and was used only for grazing the horses. Reputedly a doctor who had once lived at the manor had used the field for burying his 'mistakes', and there were thought to be many bodies in the ground there.

However, the ghostly goings-on at Northcoate Manor did not centre around that sad little cemetery but involved the house and its sweeping gravel driveway. At about the same time each year near Christmastime, footsteps are heard scrunching loudly up the gravel driveway and approaching the front door. When the door is opened, no one is ever seen, except once when a man dressed in a long dark cloak and hat was briefly glimpsed. This appears to be some sort of recording from the past, as does another story told by Debbie.

Her bedroom was one of many in the large house and faced others across the upstairs hallway. As she was settling down to sleep late one night one of her cousin's dogs began to howl loudly, and her room suddenly became very cold. She heard a woman's footsteps coming along the corridor, accompanied by the swishing sound of a long skirt. The sound was quite distinctive and Debbie was very frightened as she knew that everyone was in bed and long since asleep.

In the morning her cousin's parents, whose room was on the other side of the corridor, also reported hearing the mystery woman. This was not the first time they had remarked on this ghostly echo from the past. An older daughter who lived in the house had become so frightened by the ghost's noisy activities that she refused to sleep alone in her room even though she was in her thirties.

Talking about these experiences reminded Debbie of an almost forgotten event in her childhood. She had been staying near Sutton Coldfield where there were some dark and unfriendly woods which, she had been told, the local people rarely visited. Overcome by temptation she had set off for a walk there, and found herself being pelted with small stones. The rain of stones was persistent and appeared to come from nowhere. They just came 'zinging through the trees', was how she put it, and at the time she thought it must be birds dropping the missiles. Much later, when she saw a programme about a poltergeist and its stone-throwing antics she wondered whether such a force could have been at work in those woods near Sutton Coldfield.

The Glowing Hand

The following case was related to me by twin brothers who lived near Preston in a house they moved to when they were sixteen. It is situated near the site of the 1649 Battle of Preston and is over 200 years old. Ghostly activity on and around old battle grounds is not uncommon and much has been written on the subject.

The first thing the family heard were odd thumping sounds that seemed to come from within the wall while the exact location was hard to pinpoint. Strange shadows were also seen, of what appeared to be objects floating across the bedrooms at night. On one occasion a curtain rail that did not exist was seen above a bed, perhaps some sort of vision from the past.

The most frightening event was when one of the brothers woke with a jolt in the early hours of the night to see a strange hand-like shape which was emitting a green glow hovering above his bed for a few seconds. Immediately afterwards he felt an overwhelming presence and a sense of sadness in the room.

As time went on the visitations became fewer, but did not cease entirely. The family have grown accustomed to such goings-on and no longer jump out of bed to turn on the lights. But they have been unable to come up with any rational explanation for the odd events.

The Plaza Poltergeist

Arthur is now in his seventies, a highly intelligent man who lists reading the works of Shakespeare and writing plays as his hobbies. In his younger days he worked as a cinema projectionist and fondly remembers his time at the Plaza cinema in Northampton where his boss was a diminutive and eccentric Scotsman named Charlie. Charlie ran the cinema almost singlehandedly, cleaning it inside and out, sticking up posters, scrubbing the entrance steps and generally doing every job he could find. Arthur's impression was that he worked 18 hours a day and needed very little sleep. Often he was seen in the light of an upstairs window repairing the spools of film ready for the next day's showing. Despite his lack of height he inspired fear and respect and was a tyrannical boss who expected perfection from others as well as himself.

Unfortunately, as television gained ground many cinemas had to close, including the Plaza. Charlie was moved to the Regal where one day he was found dead in the projectionist's box. Arthur believes that Charlie's obsessive love affair with the Plaza has somehow tied him to the place even today decades after his death. He has been seen in the light of a small upstairs window on numerous occasions by those who knew him.

The building was taken over by a department store, since when it has been seriously haunted. Staff would come to work in the morning and find the stock in complete disarray although there had been no break-in. Female staff found the toilets too creepy and preferred to cross the road to the pub opposite despite the inconvenience. The toilets were located upstairs where the projection room had once been. And a shop manager once heard the sound of the old cinema organ, whereupon he left the premises in a hurry. The shop found they had too many problems, so finally they vacated the building which now houses a bank and a furniture store.

Recent attempts by Arthur to have a look around the old place have been met with a solid wall of resistance from the current staff. He feels that Charlie's ghost in some form still haunts the site, resentful of any modern usage of 'his' Plaza on which he lavished so much love and attention for years. The story as told by Arthur was written up by the local paper.

This case does not appear to meet the criteria of a haunting of the recording type. Strong emotions invested in the building by a person at the site, someone who worked there for many years, great sadness on being asked to leave, these are what have led to strong impressions of everyday activities being replayed in the building; so strong, in fact, that women workers avoided using the upstairs rooms.

The part that emotion plays in this recording process is not yet clear, but it is a common factor. Negative emotions such as fear and hate, for example, cause modern witnesses to experience distress, together with those same feelings. Animals are even more sensitive to these recordings. They are a good gauge of ghostly activity. This type of ghost does not need survival of death or a spirit form to cause the effects. All it needs is for the right conditions to be in place during a person's lifetime.

A College Initiation

On my monthly slot on Anna Murby's afternoon show with BBC Radio Northampton I generally begin by relating a couple of stories from my files, and then in the second half of the programme listeners can phone in with their own experiences or queries about ghosts and the supernatural. One day a lady called Pat told her intriguing story.

In the 1940s she had been a young student at Sheffield College. Most of the students were accommodated in a huge upstairs room with high ceilings that was partitioned off into cubicles just big enough for a bed and a dressing table.

One night Pat was woken suddenly in the small hours by a strong sense of a presence in the room. She opened her eyes to see a white silhouette-like shape gliding silently across the floor. She described its consistency as that of thick white smoke, or what she would imagine ectoplasm to look like. No really distinct details or features were visible, but it was a human shape. The spectre glided past the bed and came to rest standing by the mullioned window.

Pat rushed to the next-door cubicle where her neighbour was surprised to be disturbed, but exclaimed, 'Whatever's the matter, you look as though you've seen a ghost!' Too scared to return to her own bed, Pat ended up sharing her friend's, and indeed it was some time before she dared sleep in her own cubicle again.

At breakfast next morning the sighting was discussed and it transpired that the building was known to be haunted. After the war it had been used as a military hospital. When I spoke at greater length with Pat later she confirmed the truth of the old adage about one's hair standing on end, for that is what had happened to her that night. She felt that the presence had been that of a man. Could he have been one of the soldiers who had died in the hospital?

III

PSYCHIC EPISODES

17

Brighter Beings

On a holiday to Israel we visited the Western wall, more commonly known as the Wailing Wall. Guarded by armed soldiers, visitors flock to place prayers and messages in the small cracks in the weathered golden stone. The men approach from one side, the women from another. As usual I was carrying young Becky. She was by far the most clingy of my three children and was about four years old.

I was still suffering with fairly poor health and it was wearing me down. I wrote a prayer on the only piece of paper I could find in my bag, the back of a Macdonald's receipt. I just asked to feel better. Becky placed the scrap of paper in a crack already almost full. I knew that some people believed this place to act as a direct conduit to a higher power. Alas I had no such faith, only a vague hope. However, on our slow journey that day from Eilat to Jerusalem I was struck by a strange, mysterious quality about the old city. As we drove up the mountainous road to the city I heard an immense buzzing and humming-like sound. I asked the others if they heard it and was shocked that they couldn't. It was so loud and strong that it made my head ache. I felt this place to have very strong energies. It felt like a vast generator of energy.

Roughly two weeks after our return home I had the most vivid of dreams. In the dream I was sitting down on some grass beside a gently flowing river. The grass was quite unlike any I had ever seen, the green of it so bright and vibrant as to be almost glowing. It was of a softness too that I had never felt. Suddenly I became aware that I was not alone, for in the river stood a man. His dimensions were staggering; he stood at least eight to nine feet tall and was muscular and strong, his tanned and bronze face shining like metal. He wore a long flowing, bluish-white shift or tunic tied at the waist with a belt that looked like a snake made out of metal which moved as a real snake might. His eyes were dark, almost black, and behind him were wings so gossamer light as to be almost invisible. I can remember being afraid and in awe of this man, thinking that he could see through me and all my faults and that he had an unfathomable power. Even though he was standing in the river with the water flowing up to his mid-calves and his tunic several inches into the water, for some reason he was not getting wet. The water was flowing past him but not actually touching him.

He began to speak telling me not to be afraid and instantly the fear left me. He told me that he was there because of my interest in Israel. He said that there would always be strife in the holy city but that it would never truly be allowed to fall. He gestured with his hand showing how the city was protected. I asked him about the Palestinians. Would the Jews and Palestinians ever get on in peace? He replied that they were both from the same tree. The branches were now very separate but were fed from the same roots. Their differences were a result of human frailties and generations of war. His use of language seemed slightly strange to me. He spoke mostly using metaphors, painting pictures in my mind directly by his words. He said that the humming I picked up on the drive to Jerusalem was the original energy that was there to attract humanity and awaken our spirituality. This energy source was the reason that this small place on earth commanded such powerful religious fervour.

We spoke for a long time and then he told me it was time to leave. I asked him if I would see him again and his answer was curious and to this day I do not understand it. He replied: 'You will see us in the third light'.

I can remember waking up and feeling that I had just experienced something deeply profound. I will never forget that man in the river.

Many years later I was to have a second, briefer encounter, again via a dream, with such beings. I was going through my painful divorce, and one night as I lay in bed I felt especially vulnerable and lonely. I hated the house that I had moved to and felt that I would never feel safe again. I dreamt that I was elevated to a position slightly above the roof of my small house and was shocked to see four creatures, sitting at each corner. They had the body of an animal, something like a large cat, and the faces of men. From the centre of their backs protruded four wings. The movement of their wings was their only movement as they sat watching. Their entire bodies were uniform in colour, almost as if made from red stone, yet they seemed to be alive.

I was told that they were there to protect the house. When I eventually awoke I felt a sense of calm and peace. Then it struck me that those beings were similar to the Egyptian Sphinx. Did the ancient Egyptians envisage such beasts too? Is that indeed what the Sphinx represented – an angel on sentry duty guarding the pyramids?

I believe these two dreams gave a glimpse of another reality that overlaps our own, and has a direct hand in governing us without our being aware.

18

Three Mothers

At a bad time in my marriage I was rather glad to be asked to do a tarot reading for a young woman named Marie who lived in a beautifully kept house on a rather run-down estate. She said she had always wanted to have her fortune told but had only now got around to it. As she sat down beside me in her kitchen she let out a huge sigh.

She seemed nervous and afraid as I laid out the cards, and I found them to be full of death and suffering. I asked whether she had lost both her mother and her child. She was surprised that I knew, and her eyes filled with tears. She had married young and been happy until she had had a stillborn child. Fetching a small box from the next room she showed me a photograph of the baby with its hair brushed forward under a bonnet. It looked asleep. She had been allowed to take the picture as something to remember the little girl by. 'But my husband won't let me have the photo on display; he says it's not right, so I keep it hidden in this box like a guilty secret.' She wept as her locked emotion burst out. Then I noticed how cold the room had become, so cold that our breath was coming out as vapour although it was May and the weather was quite mild.

Near the window I saw the faint outline of a woman who looked Irish cradling a baby in her arms, rocking to comfort it.

I said to Marie, 'Your mother has the child. She's looking after her now.' And I asked whether her mother was Irish. With a smile Marie said that she was. We sat there for a while, but nothing else came up. But the room remained cold. Feeling strangely exhausted I took my leave and drove home, turning up the car heating in an attempt to get warm, but I didn't really warm up properly until I went to bed. I have never felt such cold either before or since.

Only a couple of weeks later I was asked to return to the same town to do a tarot reading for another woman, Pauline. The house was full of people who had come to see what would happen although only two of them wanted readings. Pauline introduced herself and her little son who was clinging to her legs grizzling. She said she had been feeling under the weather and was hoping for something to cheer her up. Once more the kitchen was chosen as the best place and a table had been made ready there. Pauline invited a young girl to go first, so I found myself with Debbie, her cousin, who seemed a little nervous. I did her reading, telling her all the things that came up. Then I noticed a woman standing behind Debbie and wondered how she had come in unnoticed. As I asked her to please wait her turn she laughed and said, 'Tell her I can talk now,' and then faded away very quickly. By this time Debbie had turned round to see who I was talking to but was surprised to see no one. I told her a woman bearing a strong resemblance to her had stood behind her watching us. Debbie was shocked and, pushing back her chair, left the kitchen without another word. I was quite shocked myself and thought I must have said something to upset her.

A few moments later she returned holding Pauline by the

hand. Both looked as though they had been crying. While Debbie tried to comfort Pauline I asked whether I had upset them. Pauline said, 'No, in fact you've made me feel better than I've felt in weeks.' She told me that after she had booked me to come and see her, her mother had died from a form of motor-neurone disease. In the end the muscles in her throat had been affected and she had lost the ability to speak. She had only been in her fifties and had been obviously distressed at being unable to say goodbye. 'I wanted to cancel you as I felt too upset, but my friends told me to go ahead as it might help.' Two things were remarkable, she told me. Firstly, her mother had borne a striking resemblance to Debbie and had not looked like Pauline at all. Secondly, her little boy had seen her mother in the kitchen and had said several times, 'Nana is here.' But Pauline had told him not to be silly, as Nana was in heaven with Jesus. From what I had told her, Pauline now felt that her mother had survived in some way. She hugged me, and I felt her relax.

I had a sense of having been meant to visit that house so that the mother could contact her daughter to let her know all was well. Having only been seen by her grandson whose words, understandably, had not been believed or heeded, she needed someone else as a conduit to pass on the message.

The bond between mothers and their children is the strongest one there is and survives even death. I have a very close relationship with my own mother. On one occasion I was rushing to an important meeting when I was suddenly assailed by a dreadful feeling of doom. For some reason I knew that my mother was in imminent danger, so abandoning all thought of the meeting I drove the six miles to her house at

118 | PSYCHIC QUEST

breakneck speed. As I drew up I saw my mother staggering towards me with injuries so terrible that I hardly recognized her. She looked as though she had been in a car crash. In fact she had fallen from her horse and been thrown on to the tarmac road and skidded along on her face. The doctor came within half an hour and said she needed urgent attention, so she was bundled into a car and rushed to hospital where she was found to need fifty stitches. In the end she recovered well, and when she asked me what had made me turn up at her house that evening when I didn't usually visit at that time of day, all I could say was that in a strange way I had had no choice but to follow the strongest hunch I had ever had that I was needed because something awful had happened. I'm sure she would follow her hunches if I was ever in a similar predicament.

19

Possession

A student at a London film school was making a short film about ghosts and through his work he had come into contact with Linda, a woman in her late forties who felt she was possessed by demons. Feeling her claims to be genuine and having heard of my work, the student rang and asked whether I could help. I promised to do my best although I had had very little experience with possession. Restless souls haunting a building were one thing. They could sometimes be helped to move on, but haunted people? However, I wanted to help Linda, and so I rang her up. She was quite shy at first, but gradually her story unfolded. For the past 12 months she had believed herself to have become possessed by something evil that had invaded her, something foreign to her understanding. She was also plagued by haunting-like effects in her home, strange pinpricks of light and objects going missing. I told her that all the cases of possession I had read about had come to a satisfactory end for the sufferer, omitting to mention that this was not always the case for the person performing the exorcism or 'clearance'.

Over the ensuing weeks she rang me many times and I gave her advice and encouraged her to soldier on. She was very afraid and at her wits' end, in fact on one occasion she was contemplating suicide. I persuaded her to carry on, if only for her son's sake. Her grown son lived with her but he worked long hours and was often away. I promised I would try to get to London and rid her of her tormentor. But I did admit to myself that I had grave doubts as to whether this was a genuine case of possession or whether Linda was suffering from some type of mental problem.

Then Vicky, a journalist at *Cosmopolitan,* rang me saying she had heard of my work and wondered whether I would agree to an interview for an article on possession and exorcism. I agreed, and mentioned Linda in case I might combine the interview with my visit to her. I reasoned that if I was unable to help her maybe someone reading the magazine would be able to do so. On the whole I believe that things happening together are meant to and that they are not random coincidences.

We agreed to meet at Linda's home and I was hopeful of being able to help even if only in a small way. When I got to the Underground station nearest Linda's flat she and the photographer for the interview came to collect me in his car. I was shocked by her appearance. Her grey hair was scraped back from a pretty but careworn face and she certainly looked like a person haunted. Vicky arrived at the same time and seemed very interested in Linda's story, listening patiently. The angle the magazine wanted to explore was that possession and exorcism still take place in the modern world but that people shy away from talking about it.

I had asked Linda on the phone whether she had any objects that were unusual or that she had acquired prior to the haunting. She now showed us a small Egyptian sarcophagus a friend had brought back from Egypt some years before. She doubted that it was even a genuine relic. Since speaking to me she had kept it in her garden shed. When she handed it to me I was surprised by its size and weight, for it was only about 12 inches long yet very heavy. It appeared to be made of stone such as black marble, and an exquisite carving on its lid depicted a pharaoh holding a child. The lid slid back to reveal a small cavity which had contained a little carved mummy effigy. This was lost, but Linda said this had happened several times before and it usually turned up unexpectedly.

Handling the sarcophagus I was struck by the feeling of malevolence and death it emitted. I thought it was genuine and sensed that it had once been buried deep in the sand. I also felt that the stone from which it was carved was part of a temple that had fallen, the materials being re-used to make religious objects. Since I feel that it is extremely unlucky and in a way disrespectful to possess such funerary objects, I wondered whether this relic might indeed by the cause of Linda's haunting.

Linda looked at me gravely when I told her my thoughts, and some of what I was saying appeared to be sinking in. Vicky offered to ask her sister, who worked at the British Museum, to have a look at the sarcophagus, and we both suggested that Linda might donate it to a museum since its removal might effect a cure if the possession was indeed connected with her ownership of it. But Linda still wanted me to attempt an exorcism as she felt the problem was within herself.

In the half hour I spent with Linda I got the strong impression that she was not possessed at all, but rather that the problem lay outside her in her immediate environment. I found more proof of this later when we went up to her bedroom. The curtains were drawn and in the semi-darkness we saw tiny dancing pinpricks of light near the wardrobe. In one of his books Albert Budden has written about this phenomenon which is found in locations that are electro-magnetic hotspots. Linda's flat could easily qualify for this since it is quite close to a power station. Although I tried to explain my thoughts, Linda remained convinced that she was possessed, even though I pointed out that any spirit would have manifested and become angry when I told it to move on. Whenever I made a practical suggestion to Linda as to what she might do to help herself she found a reason not to do it. My parting advice was to get rid of the sarcophagus and try to move house. But she was worn down by her circumstances and apathetic to change. I knew that there was nothing I would be able to do that would help her if she couldn't or wouldn't at least attempt to help herself.

Some of the people one visits in the course of an investigation are likely to be suffering from a mental illness of some sort. Stories like Linda's are usually written off as delusional, but this is not true in all cases. However, an actual haunting and subsequent distress can indeed lead on to a mental illness.

20

Phantoms of the Radio

BBC Radio Northampton, my local station, has regularly given me opportunities to talk about my books and appeal for new stories. For a while I even had a monthly spot on the afternoon show. Some of the stories people told were fascinating and well worth a follow-up visit both to the person and the place. The building that houses the radio station also had its own ghost which I found out about one summer's afternoon when Paul and Sue Hopgood were talking about their house and its poltergeist outbreak, after which it would be my turn to speak. The presenter was a true sceptic who scoffed openly. Although his teasing was light-hearted, I could tell that Paul and Sue were annoyed. I was sitting with others in the waiting area when suddenly the room became incredibly cold. I asked the trainee who was making coffee for us whether she could turn off the air-conditioning since it was rather fierce, but she said, 'We don't have any here.' When my turn came to go on air, Paul and Sue took seats in the waiting area. After I had answered some questions the lines were opened for the phone-in for people to ask questions or tell their own tales. As I was taking the first call, the lines went dead, and the only sound was a high-pitched whistling. All I could do was apologize. Paul and Sue told me that while they were waiting they had picked up on the spirit of an elderly woman who haunted the place. She had been cross at the presenter's sceptical tone and decided to stop the show by interfering with the phone lines.

My father had heard the broadcast and when I got home he rang to ask what I had done to the phone system. He always pulls my leg about my seeming ability to cause mayhem when in the vicinity of electrical equipment, but in this instance I told him I didn't think it could have been me. Two days later he rang again saying that on tuning in to Radio Northampton he had heard that their phone lines were still not working and they had had to cancel the gardening phone-in. I feared that my radio days were over, but I need not have worried, since I've been a regular pretty much ever since.

Some of the callers have had fascinating stories to tell, many of them for the first time. A woman driving home late at night was negotiating a roundabout when she felt the presence of someone in the back of the car. Glancing in the mirror she was horrified to see the headless figure of a man sitting on the back seat. She stopped immediately and turned round to look physically, but there was no one there. Shakily she drove home and blurted out the story to her surprised husband. He believed her because he had heard that a man had quite recently been decapitated in an accident at that very roundabout. The woman told me that although her experience had happened some time ago, she was still too afraid to use that route.

Then there was the writer on military history. He had visited a Second World War cemetery in Belgium several times. On one occasion he had gone there in mid-July when the weather was almost uncomfortably hot. He had been standing beside the grave of a young boy, Reuben, when all of a sudden the temperature dropped sharply, so much so in fact that he could see his breath coming out as vapour. Then he heard the voices of a man and a woman laughing; their feet were crunching on the gravel path. He looked round as they got closer, but there was no one to be seen, and what was more, all the paths were either earthen or wooden and not gravel. He was certain he had been in the presence of ghosts.

A man asked whether inanimate objects could become haunted, and I confirmed that they can, mentioning cases of afflicted armchairs, paintings, cars and even an oak blanket box. He told me he had been having problems since acquiring a mirror for his bedroom. But when he told me he had bought it a couple of years ago at a popular chain store I had to laugh, reassuring him that haunted objects always have a long history behind them.

There was the sad case of a man who rang on behalf of his mother who had been terrified by a ghost. Her own mother had drowned herself in a fit of depression, and it appeared that she had briefly returned to visit her daughter. But instead of comfort the visit had caused distress. I assured the son that visits from deceased loved ones are not uncommon, but that many people do not like to talk about them for fear of ridicule. In most cases a visit is a great comfort to the bereaved. I told him to reassure his mother that it was unlikely his grandmother would come again and it was likely that her visit was a way of saying goodbye.

Not all callers ring up about ghosts. Some are ardent disbelievers who like to ring and pour scorn on the work I do.

Everyone should be entitled to express opinions both for and against the existence of ghosts, and these calls add balance to the programme. But I must admit that sometimes such people leave me hot under the collar.

21

Reading the President's Palm

A satellite television company asked me to take part in a programme on palmistry. I had worked with them before and they were impressed by my psychic ability. And they knew I relish a challenge. When I first met the team one of the cameramen was sceptical saying he didn't believe in 'all that psychic stuff'. He challenged me to tell him something about himself which only he and no one else knew. After thinking for a moment I replied, 'I can tell you something only you and your girlfriend know. You often tease her about her odd-shaped toes. You love them but you tease her nevertheless.' Scratching his chin he exclaimed, 'Wow, how did you know that?'

The producer then asked me to do the same with her. I was ready, as I had intended to take her aside later because I had picked up that the wiring in her new house was dangerous, an accident waiting to happen, especially in the bathroom and shower. The former owner had done the wiring on the cheap, and I asked her whether he had been a Scot. She was astonished that I knew she had recently moved and promised to have all the wiring checked by a competent electrician. The former owner had indeed been a Scot and a DIY enthusiast.

People often ask me where I get my information from. I can only conclude that most comes from picking up on thoughts and worries of people I meet, and for some reason it is even stronger with strangers or those I don't know very well. The rest must come from the spirit world, for the spirits do take a close interest in the everyday goings on in our lives. They watch out for us and try to warn us of impending danger and disaster. If they use me as a conduit for their messages I am happy to oblige. So many people do not listen or do not even know how to.

The programme was about my interpretation of a newspaper report about Prime Minster Tony Blair's palm. A palmist had noticed from a close-up photograph that he had a simian line, one which is said to be prevalent in criminals and also in people with Down's syndrome. The programme makers wanted me to deduce from the photo as much as I could about our country's leader. I suggested that while we were about it, why not read the Conservative Party opposition leader William Hague's palm and President Bill Clinton's as well. So I obtained close-up photos of all these men's hands.

Obviously this was all quite light-hearted, but I was surprised how much I learnt. Tony Blair's palm was strongly defined. Here was a man who liked his own way and got it. He had a highly developed intuitive nature, going with his hunches which were usually right. This gave him an advantage over his peers. He could often guess the actions and reactions of others and had used this skill to rise to the very top. The strong lines on his hand pointed to a person destined to lead, but he would not lead alone as Margaret Thatcher had before him. He needed the input and support of those around him, especially his wife, who is mentally superior to him, and he knows it.

William Hague has rather feminine hands. From the weakness in his palm I predicted beforehand that losing the election would lead to his resignation. He is a decent and honest man but easily defeated.

Then I turned to Bill Clinton's hands with relish. He has the large, beefy hands of someone with a huge appetite for life and everything in it. We all know about his sexual indiscretions during his presidency, for which most people forgave him. He finds it hard to control his appetite for the pleasures in life, as witness his tendency to put on weight. He will never be able to change this. His hands also show his strong leadership qualities which were demonstrated even as he rushed to the devastation of the World Trade Centre in New York, getting there sooner even than President Bush. He has a strongly caring nature, and his concern for his country at that time spoke volumes. He has probably found it hard to hand over the reins to another man.

All this was of course not the same as actually meeting the three men in question and doing a proper reading of their actual palms. Perhaps they would like to contact me, and I shall be pleased to read their palms properly!

22

Phantom Disappointments and Meetings

Ghost-hunting could be described as being 10% hope, 80% disappointment and 10% getting genuine, worthwhile evidence. But it is worth it. There is nothing I would rather do than sit around in cold, draughty locations losing many a night's sleep, and I can see myself still doing it in my seventies and eighties. No report of my investigations would be complete without some of the failures — cases that sounded promising but proved to be damp squibs, witnesses who were mistaken in what they had seen or else deliberately set out to mislead me or, more commonly, simply misunderstandings.

The first time this happened was when my sister-in-law mentioned a friend who knew someone who worked as a housekeeper in a haunted house. When I reached the lady on the phone I explained that I was writing a book on ghosts and wondered whether she would share her experiences with me. Sounding slightly bemused, she said that she didn't have any, but her neighbour had three in the garden, so perhaps I should talk to her. It turned out that she thought I was talking about goats, and she denied any knowledge of ghosts in the house where she worked. After that I tried not to raise my hopes that there would be a good story, for most often there is nothing there.

Instances of being deliberately misled also occur. A man

The beautiful church ruins at Boughton Green, Northamptonshire

The picture created for the cover of my first book

Photos: Patrick Leonard

sent me a photo of a ghostly semi-transparent figure sitting on a sofa. It looked too good to be true, which was what it turned out to be. The sender had been teasingly trying to scare his children by telling them their house was haunted, and he had taken this double exposure of himself as the ghost.

I know how easy it is to do this as I have done it myself, for the cover of my book *Walking through Walls*. I needed an evocative cover shot for what was my first ever brush with the literary world, so I decided to create my own in the haunted churchyard at Boughton in Northamptonshire. It is a beautiful, neglected place with dramatic trees and ivy entwining the broken and crooked gravestones. Patrick photographed me dressed up in a long Victorian dress with a knitted shawl and lace-up boots. I always show this photo when I give a lecture. People sometimes gasp and shudder, taking it to be real, but my purpose is to demonstrate that quite realistic photos can be faked, and that any serious investigator must insist on seeing the negative in order to rule out the old double exposure trick.

Pictures of ghosts sometimes appear in the daily press. Unfortunately most of these have turned out to be fakes, though not all. The lure of money is tempting, as is the thought of getting one over on an unsuspecting public. I always try to use a Polaroid camera when interviewing or mounting an investigation as any results captured on such a camera are harder to refute. However, to satisfy the scientists we shall in the future have to produce photographs under strict laboratory conditions.

Meanwhile, there is also a body of photographic evidence whose provenance has not been disputed.

*

When you are psychic or clairvoyant, meeting others who are similarly psychically aware can engender mixed feelings. On the one hand it is comforting to meet someone who, like yourself, partially depends on information received from 'outside', because people who don't share your insight often see you as scary or a freak and this makes you feel isolated. On the other hand there can be a kind of rivalry between psychics as to whose ability is the strongest. A most disappointing experience is meeting fraudulent mediums who charge high prices for generalistic platitudes given out under false pretences. On the few occasions when people have come for readings and I have received no information I have simply not charged them. They may have been cross, but I would prefer not to deceive them.

Two impressive mediums I have come to know quite well are Paul and Sue Hopgood whom I first met when I went to interview them about their long-running poltergeist outbreak. That was an event which changed their lives in that it not only put them in touch with their spiritual side but also made them discover that they both had considerable artistic talent. Sue says her pictures of people and places 'just come to her'. They had nicknamed their poltergeist Fred. I twice witnessed Fred's work, once when a small coffee table moved about on its own, and a second time when we heard a noise from the kitchen and rushed in to find not only all the cupboard doors open but also numerous kitchen utensils arranged in sculpture-like piles. We had left the kitchen only minutes before, and anyone else would have taken some time to achieve the same effect. There was also a feeling of electricity in the air as before a storm, a feeling that something 'other' had just vacated the spot. Paul and Sue have predicted many things in my life.

Two other psychics I know would probably scoff if you told them they possessed such abilities. One is my father whose secretary pointed out to him that he only needed to talk about someone and that person would phone him. 'Just try it', she said. He did, and immediately received a call from the person. After that he used the ploy many times, which perhaps even kept his business ticking over, and he finds it happens even now that he has retired.

The other is the actor Anthony Quinn whom I met in New York. He was very coy when I asked him whether he was psychic. He just laughed and replied that he was not, but that he was a democrat...

*

I would like to mention here a meeting with a life-long hero of mine, the author Laurie Lee. I met him at a writer's gathering in London held in a large oak-panelled room. The champagne flowed and waiters served an assortment of canapés. It was a well-attended event with all kinds of writers, including such luminaries as Jilly Cooper and Claire Rayner. I had taken along a copy of one of Laurie Lee's books, which I hoped he would sign for me. The room was noisy and full to bursting but I spotted him sitting alone in the corner. I went over and asked if he minded if I sat next to him. 'Not at all', he replied with a smile. Although he was someone I had always wanted to meet since reading his *Cider with Rosie* at school, I was not nervous. I told him how much I loved his work and that I had named my son Laurie after him. He held my hand gently and looked into my eyes, his own moist with tears. We discussed writing, and he expressed amazement that *Cider with Rosie* had never been out of print since it was first published all those years ago. I told him not to be so surprised as most people can recognize greatness in something when they read it. It is a cliché, but it felt as if we were the only people in the room.

Soon it was time for me to go and I promised Laurie a copy of my book, which I sent him. Sadly he only had a few more weeks to live. His death filled me with great sorrow, but I was so blessed to have met him. To me he is one of the greatest writers of the twentieth century, for he paints such a vivid picture of rural Britain with a lightness of touch that at times takes one's breath away. He found beauty in the smallest things and portrayed his feeling through his writing. I will always treasure the book he signed for me.

23

Developing Psychic Abilities

I strongly believe that we all have some degree of psychic ability, although most of us do not realize this, whether it be a businessman's gut feeling before closing a deal or a mother's odd feeling that she should go and check on her child. My friend Patrick Leonard is a case in point. He professes to having no psychic ability, yet he regularly predicts things, saying afterwards that it was just a fluke. A fluke can happen once or twice, but never on a regular basis.

Perhaps we have largely lost our powers of intuition through lack of use. Nowadays we use the telephone to contact our loved ones. Most people would be 'lost' without their mobile phone. But our ancient ancestors had no such luxury. They survived and communicated with each other largely through their wits and physical energy, but I think they also communicated and survived danger by using their psychic energies.

The first step in developing one's psychic powers is to utilize dreams. Most of us on waking will remember a snippet of the content of a dream. It is useful to keep a dream diary by the bed so that on waking you can immediately write down any impressions gained during sleep. You may only be able to remember enough to jot down a few words, but this doesn't matter. As time goes on your recall of dreams will improve.

The reason why this is important is because in sleep the mind can act unfettered and unrestrained by the logical processes of brain function.

It is the intellectual functions that kill off any attempts at working in the psychic sphere. You are at an advantage if you are of an artistic, creative disposition because you are then already halfway there. Your mind is governed by the creative side of your brain. After a few weeks' practice you should notice how some of the material in your dreams corresponds with situations, conversations and happenings later on. I believe that when we sleep we have full access to the events of our past and some extent the future. Scientists have discovered that time appears not to be linear, as had previously been supposed, but rather more complicated. We consider it to be a sequence of 'nows'; we pass from one 'now' to the next for the whole of our lives, with access to the past in memories but to the future in hopes alone. In the world of the atom, however, there is no past, no now and no future. Everything is happening at the same time.

Another use for your dreams lies in practical problem solving. This has worked for me on many occasions, but one in particular comes to mind. When we were married and living in our old house we wanted to remove a very large armchair but could not get it through the door whichever way we tried. Having struggled all day, I went to bed thinking we would have to leave it where it was. But then I dreamt exactly how to angle the chair to get it out, and to everyone's amazement the next day we were able to shift it.

I find that dream problem solving works best with small, irritating, seemingly intractable problems such as the above.

Over the years it has proved very useful. The secret is to think over the problem before falling asleep. It may take several nights before any answer materializes, but it's well worth trying and you have nothing to lose.

Another way to develop your psychic ability is to follow what we term gut feelings and see what happens. Was there a reason for that feeling? In most cases perhaps there wasn't, but for your abilities to develop you have to trust in your own instincts. This takes time, so be patient.

The next step is visualization. Spend some time each day sitting quietly and empty your mind of all the day's thoughts and clutter. This has two benefits. Firstly it is relaxing and secondly you may find thoughts and information springing in and filling the void. This state of total 'unthinking' is how I always try to be when working psychically. I imagine my brainwaves flattening out.

Psychometry is another good area to try. This involves the reading of objects. I have had some good success at this myself and it is fun. Children seem to be particularly good at it. The theory behind psychometry is that objects store information, particularly if they are regularly handled or worn. Therefore jewellery and watches are good articles to try out. One way of testing your powers is to have a friend take several objects and place them in sealed envelopes, so they must be flat things such as a newspaper cutting, a birthday card, cinema ticket or letter perhaps. The friend folds each one inside a piece of plain paper and seals it in an envelope. You have to see how many you can guess correctly. Most of the time you will just get a faint impression or words. Go with this, for our first impressions are usually right.

When I have read people's palms in the past I have felt that only a small proportion of the information I receive is via the imprint of the lines. Most is due to reading the person through holding their hand. I am sure that if they simply laid their hand on the table and I had no physical contact with them I would be almost useless.

One incident springs to mind. I was asked to read the hand of a man who outwardly looked to be in robust health. Almost instantly my mind picked up a picture of a diseased-looking human kidney. Then I saw a glass of water. I asked the man whether he had a problem with his kidneys and told him he should drink more water. One of his problems was that he didn't drink enough, which was putting a strain on his kidneys. His reply was, 'Have you been talking to my doctor?' Of course I had never met his doctor but had picked up the information simply by holding the man's hand. I had not even got around to studying the palm.

You will no doubt find that the more you work on your psychic ability the stronger it will grow. Most highly psychic people find that their powers vary enormously at different periods in their life. This certainly applies to me. At times I have felt almost powerless and at others that I could achieve anything I wanted. As your ability grows you will feel more connected with your fellow human beings. No one is an island, and if you succeed in picking up on another's thoughts you will realize that the barriers we erect around ourselves are useless.

Conclusions

This book draws on a lifetime of experience and years of research in the field of ghosts. However, to those of you who feel you might want to follow in my footsteps I must repeat that it is a field littered with disappointments. On most occasions when I have visited potential paranormal 'hotspots' absolutely nothing has happened. Ghost investigators and members of the Ghost Club who are trying to gather evidence go prepared to be disappointed. One does not strike lucky very often. During the nights I have spent sitting around in draughty old buildings and empty pubs the most activity has frequently been the odd light going on or off by itself, or an object changing its position in the dark.

However, it is good fun, and you do get to know the most interesting individuals. When first meeting people in their home following a tip-off about a possible haunting, the primary object is to put them at their ease about the situation. It is very rare that the ghost phenomenon can cause any harm. Yet many people are afraid when they see a ghost and feel that their home has been invaded. If allowed to persist, the fear itself can cause real physical illness. Except in rare circumstances, apparitions themselves cannot do harm.

I do not claim to be an expert, but merely an enthusiastic observer and collector of data about people and places. You might call me an enthusiastic amateur in my chosen field of research, someone who is learning all the time. What I can pass on to others is what I have discovered, especially in the past 10 years or so. So it will be up to readers to draw their own conclusions.

*

The smallest category in any investigator's caseload, but the one that gets the most attention, is the malevolent ghost. This is the only type that can, potentially, harm an individual. Some poltergeists, but not all, fall into this group. 'Poltergeist', as I mentioned earlier, is German for 'noisy spirit'. It is an apt name. The following criteria are usually set out to describe this phenomenon and the conditions that cause it to arise. Many eminent psychologists, scientists and fellow researchers believe this to be true:

1. There is an adolescent, pubescent or prepubescent youngster living in the house.
2. There is disharmony in the family group (divorce, depression, severe arguments).
3. There is economic hardship.

Some or all of these indicators are found to be present in homes experiencing a poltergeist outbreak. However, I find focussing on this set of pointers unhelpful since it in no way covers all the circumstances I have come across on my travels or the cases I have read about. Many have none of these criteria present. So we have to look elsewhere for some of the answers although most experts in this field put the phenomenon squarely at the door of 'telekinesis'.

The scenario involves a pubescent youngster, frustrated and unhappy, causing mayhem in the home. It is seen as an unintentional, subconscious cry for help, a burst of psychic energy at a time when there is a confusion of sexual hormones and change. If the child is indeed very mixed up it is easy to see what an attractive theory this is if you believe in telekinesis. Everything seems to fit, and there is indeed a body of research going back to the early part of the century which tells of individuals who are able to move small objects in laboratory conditions. This has even been filmed.

Although I believe that telekinesis is possible, I think that it is only part of the picture. Once you have set aside the hoaxers and attention seekers you are left with quite a lot more to ponder about, and I have come to the conclusion that some poltergeist outbreaks have more to them than this. They happen all over the world and can occur in all kinds of family groupings or even where only one individual is involved. Our world really does seem to consist of many dimensions and sometimes various forces seem to be in competition with each other for the available space. I am sure that our minds and spirits do survive even death.

Our brains are much more than a cluster of cells, nerves and fibres and it is possible for our thoughts to escape the confines of the skull and affect people and things around us. Quantum physics tells us that the observer in an experiment can affect the outcome at the molecular level. The course of an atom can be changed by the expectations of the scientist conducting the experiment. So if the mind can escape the confines of the body, in however small a way, then surely the death of that body is no barrier to the ongoing activities of that mind. Perhaps it can go on thinking, feeling and affecting matter indefinitely. Most of the major religions of the world preach some form of survival after death. It is my strong belief that this fact of survival can play a part in malevolent hauntings. It is entirely possible that such cases could be caused by the living on of a part of an evil or intensely negative person's mind intent on invading the space occupied by others. This space could be a home, a workplace or even the site of that individual's death.

In my experience, the good or positive always overcomes the bad or negative in the end. That is why the poltergeist phenomenon is quite often temporary. It is as though such hauntings involve an invisible battle of wills for territory both physical and emotional. Perhaps this even accounts for examples throughout history of supposed demonic possession; perhaps we are not possessed by demons but by the former living.

Other groups of malevolent or negative hauntings could well be due, in part at least, to environmental factors and triggers. Our earth as we know it is one vast magnet and has in its crust many cracks and fissures. At times of stress between the tectonic plates these can release poisonous gases. Also, flowing underneath the ground are many rivers and streams, and water has a strong effect on electrical fields. These naturally occurring substances and forces – electrical, magnetic and hydrodynamic – affect us all, both human and animal. Many people feel depressed and have a headache before a thunderstorm, only to be refreshed and miraculously alert once the storm breaks. Others are affected by the cycles of the moon or changing weather patterns. Those suffering from schizophrenia are said to feel much improved when it is raining. There are doctors in Spain using simple magnets to treat depression in the mentally ill, raising hopes that in the future such treatments might replace more invasive drug and ECT therapies.

So, invisible forces that surround us quite naturally can and do affect our mood both for good and bad. If some buildings or locations have all the necessary criteria to enable all of these aspects to come together we could call that space a naturally occurring hotspot. Such a place would have distinct possibilities of disturbance for both humans or animals residing or visiting there. Let us imagine a location with all the following circumstances: high-tension cables directly overhead, bedrock with weaknesses and faults, an underground stream or river. These three factors could cause a home to become an area of negative energies, albeit mostly naturally occurring. Strong electrical and magnetic fields in a building could predispose sensitive inhabitants to feel very negative eventually.

Looked at in another way, we could consider a dreadful event such as a murder, suicide or fatal accident taking place at a location or in a building that was able in some way to record a part of the sounds and emotions involved. In future that could affect those visiting or residing in that place. They might see the characters involved in the drama, or hear the noises, or perhaps merely pick up on some of the negative vibrations. I believe that places where suicide is frequent, such as Beachy Head in Sussex, are a case in point and can become haunted by the despair of all those sad souls who have jumped to their death.

These are just a few of the ways in which ghosts can be harmful, cause ill health or, on rare occasions, even death. Fortunately this type of phenomenon is by far the smallest group that any researcher like myself is likely to come across.

*

The existence of mediumship and psychic faculties is still disputed by many. Others who admit to the possibility condemn it out of so-called religious conviction, thinking that such 'talents' are evil and counter to Christian teaching. Others feel that such faculties when manifesting spontaneously in a person are only right and proper if they are used under the guidance of that individual's Christian faith, e.g. the gifts of premonition, healing and contact with anything outside the earthly plane. I can understand this reasoning since there are certain passages in the Bible which condemn such practices. But I do regard this rigid view as somewhat unfair for several reasons, not least because Jesus himself possessed all these gifts and used them extensively for the good of his fellow men and women and also taught his friends and disciples how to use them.

Furthermore, we all seem to have these talents given to us at birth, more strongly in some but possibly latent in the rest of us, ready to be developed. If they are used for the good, then there should be no question of any evil or bad results from this type of work.

My friend Gary Stock is a spiritualist medium who manifests strong powers. His greatest wish is to resolve the distress that can be a consequence of a malevolent outbreak or possession. In his work he has come across voodoo curses laid on teenagers, and houses made uninhabitable by the antics of poltergeists. With bravery and common sense he has tackled such cases, ridding homes of malevolent entities with the help of holy water, prayer and faith. He tries his utmost to resolve such situations, having many successes but also failures, which are a hard lesson. How can any disbeliever say that Gary is wrong to try and help his neighbours in this way? Perhaps such abilities are like muscles which grow bigger and better the more we stretch and exercise them so that we can trust them more and more if necessary.

Mediumship is a different matter altogether, being granted only to a precious minority. This ability is more like a design fault in the engine powerhouse of the brain. You could say that individuals lacking this ability have the curtains drawn across the windows of the mind shutting out the parallel dimension that impinges on our own. Mediums, on the other hand, lack these curtains altogether, which is why this area can be so hotly disputed by the disbelievers. It is a case of the have-nots against the haves. Mediumship comes with a price, for such individuals often suffer with ill health. They seem able to help others, especially the bereaved, but count the cost of it themselves in mental strain and exhaustion. The mind is such a tremendous and complicated thing that as yet no one fully understands its workings. Scientists postulate that we only use a fraction of our brain to full capacity, a mere portion that leaves a great deal to spare. It is just possible that some part of this spare capacity of the brain is for the psychic powers of telepathy, telekinesis, premonitions and so on.

The usage of that aspect of the brain has been slowly extinguished over thousands of years as human beings have advanced in the logical areas while detaching themselves from nature, thus turning more into machines than animals. But now this long trend seems to be reversing. More and more of us are becoming interested in developing these gifts and our abilities grow if left on their own when given a free rein. But there is no way of quantifying or proving genuine psychic abilities in ways that would convince sceptics. There is a small body of research into clairvoyance, remote viewing and tele-kinesis that has yielded proof beyond reasonable doubt under laboratory conditions. But there are far fewer hits than misses when it comes to proof, so at present sceptics have the edge over the believers.

When a psychic person fails to 'perform' under test condi-tions it is usually said that nervousness and pressure to 'deliver' drive out any likelihood of success. Unlike study and revision for exams where the conscious mind is focussed, psychic skills are easier to bring to bear when the brain is on autopilot, and this is difficult when one is under pressure.

*

The most common type of ghost is the 'stone tape-recording' type, so an investigator will examine this possibility first if genuine phenomena have occurred. Such ghosts, however, cannot interact with those who witness them, for they are no more 'real' than a hologram, a television picture or a three-dimensional photograph. They are moments of past actions frozen in time sometimes more and sometimes less realisti-cally. Such 'ghosts' cannot be conjured up in laboratory con-ditions. I have come across cases where the apparition appears to be a semi-transparent monochrome in shades of grey and without any other colour. Then there are hauntings so realistic and colourful that no one would suspect the vision to be anything other than physical reality. Science is only just beginning to understand that all these variations are possible and how they might come about.

What our ancestors only a century ago would have deemed magic is all very ordinary to us: we take it for granted that we can record music on tape or listen to our children's baby voices when they have grown to be teenagers, or watch ourselves enjoying a holiday long after the sun-tan has faded. Magnetic tape records vibrations and film picks up particles of light and colour. It is possible that buildings can act in this way. Bricks and stone contain quartz and other minerals similar to those present in cassette tape and camera film. In addition, we are surrounded by magnetic fields. So some, at least, of the components needed to create a recording are present.

It is a real mystery why such recordings occur only in some buildings and then only in some of the rooms. Although ghosts can appear both in images and sounds, sounds are the most common, the usual being footsteps, banging, crying, screaming and conversation. Conversation is rarely above a whisper and barely comprehensible, so this is very annoying to the occupants of a house. A TV programme recently featured research into a pub where staff had for years been hearing all the normal pub sounds late at night long after the last customer had gone home. The researchers attached sensitive electrodes that record sound to the thick walls of the building and were rather pleased with the results they listened to next day. Captured on their tape recorders were conversations, the chink of glasses, laughter and even the dull click of dominoes, all recorded in the hours after the pub had closed when only the researchers were present. Of course this is only one example, but it chimes in nicely with the many haunted public houses I have visited over the last four years.

Other hauntings of the 'stone tape-recording' type appear to start up only when extensive renovation work is done on a property with walls being knocked down or a lot of hammering on the walls and disruption to the interior. Perhaps a wielded hammer unlocks hidden secrets in the core of a stone wall? If only this could be more fully understood, the implications for historians and archaeologists would be huge.

By tapping on the 'switch' they could listen in on the past. Many ancient buildings would reveal their secrets. The conversations of those who had lived there long ago would yield invaluable insights into our history that mere relics cannot show. Dialects long forgotten would be heard anew. Extra pieces of the jigsaw puzzle of our long heritage would be slotted into place. Even simple items like clay pots would offer this potential. Perhaps the words of the potter and the sounds around him while he worked would also have been encoded into the clay which, after all, has all the properties that exist in brick and stone.

Of course this is all a theory at present, but an exciting one nevertheless and, I sincerely hope, a distinct possibility for the future.

I have met many cases of ghostly monks the majority of which have had an entirely benign presence, so that those experiencing them are usually unafraid. This is the exact opposite of the stereotype in which shadowy monks, evil and frightening, drift along dark corridors frightening anyone unlucky enough to encounter them. Other apparitions have legs missing, heads or torsos are absent, and there is a tale of a spectral pair of hands that haunts a moor. Perhaps these ghosts were 'recorded' in the first place with less attention to detail. Also it seems that over many years apparitions fade, with the most complex parts disappearing first.

Other 'ghosts' are those which we imagine, shadows on a bedroom wall, a hooded coat hanging on the back of a door perhaps, or a pile of books and toys. There was the instance of a notorious accident black spot at a bend in the road. The accidents only seemed to happen on one day in the week, and many of those involved mentioned a ghost when interviewed by the police. The scary white apparition had distracted their attention which in turn caused them to lose control of their car. Finally the police questioned the old lady who lived in the house on the corner. It transpired that she always washed her nightgown on a particular day and often forgot to take it in once it was dry, so it was left eerily flapping in the breeze all night in full view of the road.

Albert Budden, having been a believer in the paranormal, ghosts and aliens, lost his conviction entirely after discovering what he termed the 'Hutchinson Effect' which he wrote up in *The Fortean Times*. Hutchinson replicated all the bizarre effects usually attributed to poltergeists by creating strong electrical and magnetic fields in his laboratory (as I have already mentioned earlier). Budden now feels that there is a total lack of real proof of ghostly existences. His conclusion is that our homes are constantly being bombarded by the invisible forces of electricity and magnetism emitted by TV masts, power lines, microwaves, CB radio and radio hams, and all the plethora of electrical household appliances which can, on occasion, produce ghost-like effects which may cause susceptible individuals to hallucinate and see visions of ghosts or aliens. People living in hotspots of these forces can develop an allergy to electrical items. Sometimes stress can trigger a release of such energy in one quick burst, causing chaos and disruption, overloading electrical items or computers, causing them to malfunction or even explode. Glandular problems as well as depression, diabetes, migraine and various food and chemical allergies can also ensue.

As I mentioned already, I do agree with Albert's theories up to a point, but I still feel strongly that there is a spirit dimension which overlaps our own and that ghosts most definitely do exist. Nevertheless, as a researcher I have found the 'Hutchinson Effect' valuable when trying to explain some poltergeist phenomena.

No discussion on ghosts is complete without mentioning the phenomenon regularly reported to me by perfectly sane, rational people: animal phantoms. The most commonly seen animals are dogs and cats, but horses also feature with or without a rider. I have heard of a Roman soldier with his horse, a 'stone age' man with his shaggy steed and an elegant lady riding sidesaddle.

Cats are often seen around the place where they used to live rather than at the site of their death. One example is of a small boy who was photographed on holiday six weeks after losing his much loved white kitten. He has a toy bunny in one hand and there, for all to see, in his other hand is the fluffy white face of the kitten.

Dogs frequently make a brief appearance after they have died. My sensible mother had such an experience with a dog of hers even after she had moved house. One night she felt a dog jump on to the end of her bed, just as the dog who had died used to do, and my mother stroked him for a long time before falling into a deep and satisfying sleep. Next morning her sceptical husband put it all down to a dream or hallucination brought on by grief and the stress of the move. But I believe Mum when she says that she definitely saw and stroked her dog, for she is an honest and levelheaded person.

Ghostly black dogs, not always friendly, are seen all over Britain. They are often noticed running near rivers and streams, but also in graveyards and at crossroads. Some think that their presence near a graveyard protects it from evil. The researcher Ivan Bunn feels that damp places have always played a significant part in this phenomenon. Such dogs are also seen traversing along well-known leylines and at places with naturally strong magnetic forces such as stone circles and standing stones. Such sightings are so common that I believe many place names refer to them, for example the many 'Black Lion' pubs. Some such dogs have even been known to accompany lone or frightened travellers and show them the way when they have become lost.

There are many reported sightings of animals that are out of place, such as the 'Surrey puma' and Britain's much quoted wallaby population. While I believe that most of these are real animals which have escaped from zoos or private collections and are doing well in the wild, I do think that some are spectral black cats which will therefore never be caught or leave any real clues as to their existence. I think that these may have been real exotic pets that have escaped and then died, but reappear in life – like a recording. Or they may never have existed as real-life animals, coming instead from another dimension that parallels our own.

Another phenomenon is the way pets seem to be psychic, picking up and seeing ghosts before we do. Their senses of smell, sight and hearing are much stronger than ours. Also they are low to the ground and therefore more likely to feel a sudden unexpected draught or even a leak of gas through the floor. Their sight is entirely different from ours, and also they do not judge what they see as we do, but simply see it as something real and, depending on their character, either bark, ignore it or creep away. My own dog once grew very nervous and edgy, crouching down and shivering as we approached a cottage that was reputed to be haunted.

Places of work most likely to be haunted are pubs and theatres. In the case of pubs this is easy to understand, for they are often many centuries old and have seen their fair share of death and conflict. Before modern police procedures developed, it was quite usual for the victims of accident or murder to be laid out in the pub's back room before burial, since this was the only public building available in villages and small towns. Any building associated with sudden death has the potential to become haunted. As for theatres, these are also often quite old. They are usually places of great superstition because actors are a notoriously superstitious bunch.

But ghosts are also encountered in other places of work, especially by cleaners who often have to work alone during the night. A worker in a large department store gave in his notice after a terrifying encounter with a ghost which seemed to cause a row of large mirrors to smash dramatically. The female cleaner who took his place had a similar experience, whereupon she went to the local library to find out the history of the place. She discovered that it was built over the ruins of a church and that the crypt was rumoured to have been left intact underneath.

As to my own paranormal experiences, I found the malfunctioning of electrical equipment and also metal bending to be odd in the extreme. But after a few articles about me had appeared in the press I discovered that I was by no means alone in this regard. I have had letters from as far away as New Zealand from people who presume that they, too, are living in electro-magnetic hotspots which are not only causing the effects but also having a bad effect on their health.

Finally there are the classic cases, stories that have influenced common perception and thinking about ghosts. One such is that of the Enfield poltergeist case (see Chapter 6) which was a truly terrible ordeal for the family involved as it lasted for months and could be described as malevolent. Researchers had ample time to study all aspects of the phenomenon. Virtually the whole gamut of possible aspects was available for researchers to record: levitation, teleportation, disembodied voices, trance-like states are all well documented by witnesses. Although on occasion the children involved did artificially perpetuate the activity once things had quietened down, I do believe that this was a genuine case.

As time goes by and we shed more light on the mystery, some of the fear people often feel when seeing a ghost will disappear, for fear is seldom justified. The longer I have spent researching the mystery surrounding phantoms in the British Isles the more convinced I am of their existence. The difficulty is how to define the reality of our experiences. Truth is indeed always very much stranger than fiction.

*

When I started work on this book I was a little unsure about how to proceed. Some of the things have been painful to relive and put down on paper, especially the time when I was ill and had the breakdown. But I felt that the bad times as well as the good had to be mentioned. Surviving those times and recovering from them has made me stronger. While I used to think of myself as weak I now feel that bravery is a part of my makeup, together with stubbornness, creativity and love. At last I feel that I can live with myself and be at peace with who I am. My mother is brave and has mastered many hardships, so perhaps I have carried on something from her. My paternal grandmother could be loving at one moment and terrifying the next, with a temper beyond her control. I used to dread growing up to be like her, and perhaps this has led to my propensity towards depression. Who can tell? Now, however, I have hopes for my extended family and wish that they may do well and remain friends with one another.

There are many other things I would like to do, but most of all I would like to uncover more proof of ghosts to help people stop fearing death. If I could choose one thing which I want to achieve, this is what it would be – and then my life would have been truly worthwhile.

Some Locations in the UK

Northampton, The Royal Theatre
This theatre in the town centre was opened in 1884. Although she has not been seen lately, you may be lucky enough to encounter the 'Grey Lady' while attending a play here.

Northampton, The Grosvenor Centre
This shopping centre just off Market Square has been built on the site of a former monastery and boasts at least two ghosts, a silent monk and a poltergeist in one of the shops.

Northampton, Market Square, The Shipman's Pub
This pub has remained largely unchanged over the centuries. There have been stories of a not unfriendly though mischievous ghost.

Northampton, The Wig and Pen Pub
Locals maintain that this pub is haunted, and a journalist with the local paper is known to have had a scare there. Ghostly phantoms and a spectral black dog are said to frequent the place.

Northampton, Dychurch Lane
Located a mere stone's throw from the shopping centre, this lane was the scene of a grisly murder in which a woman's head was hacked off. Locals have heard her screams.

Northamptonshire, Naseby
The famous site of a battle in the English Civil War. There are legends of battle scenes being re-enacted in the sky. Oliver Cromwell's ghost is said to haunt the place. The best time to visit is June, and wellington boots are advisable.

Northamptonshire, Ecton, The World's End Pub
There have been protracted hauntings here over the years perhaps connected with two suicides and the proximity of a hanging tree as well as the fact that the cellars were used as a morgue. Excellent food, even if the ghosts remain shy.

Northamptonshire, Higham Ferrers, The Griffin Pub
This pub was originally a row of three cottages built in 1240. A girl named Lisa, said to have been raped by Roundhead soldiers, is sometimes seen sitting in the ingle nook, and has even been mistaken for a customer.

Northamptonshire, Boughton, the churchyard and lane
In the derelict graveyard and lane below the ghost of a man ('Captain Blood') crouches menacingly and has even been said to dash out and run through or in front of cars.

Northamptonshire, Rockingham Castle
A beautiful castle with spectacular views. The scene of a murder, said to be haunted by a ghostly monk.

Northamptonshire, Salcey Forest
Haunted by the ghost of a Cavalier soldier with a thin moustache and pained expression. There have also been UFO sightings here, and on one occasion I sensed an evil miasma-

like presence. The forest has been the site of black magic and witchcraft practices.

Northamptonshire, Woodford, near Kettering, the Church
A teenager on a school project captured the spectral form of a monk kneeling at the altar, and I myself have seen this ghost, thought to be that of the Crusader Sir Walter Trayli whose heart was interred here. I have heard that this ghost has been very active recently.

London, Charlton House, Greenwich
A former manor house with beautiful architecture and fireplaces, now a public building housing a library. Many ghostly incidents over the years including a ghostly child whose bones may be those found inside a chimney, and a woman in the garden carrying a bundle. A very negative atmosphere in one of the rooms.

London, The Tower of London
Claims to be one of Britain's most haunted buildings. One famous incident concerns a soldier who saw something so terrible that he subsequently died of fright. Another was reported by several witnesses who saw a peculiar cylindrical mass traverse a room in the Keeper's Lodge.

London, Highgate Cemetery
This huge burial ground is said to be haunted not only by ghosts but also by vampires. It was made famous by the Revd Sean Manchester's tale 'The Highgate Vampire'. A string of garlic when visiting is optional.

London, Madame Tussaud's
It was here that I felt a ghostly hand touch my back. The place is eerie in its own way, whether it is haunted or not.

London, Newgate Prison
Many prisons have a dark and bloody history, and I have come across many that are haunted. The legend here was of a demonic black dog with a shuffling gait. The prison was demolished to make way for the Old Bailey.

London, 50 Berkeley Square
There does not seem to have been any trouble of a supernatural variety at this innocuous property for some time. However, a young girl is said to have been driven mad by what she saw there, and two deaths have been attributed to fright.

London, Lesnes Abbey
Tales of supernatural happenings abound at this oasis of green surrounded by a modern sprawl of suburbia. There are spectral monks, witches dancing in the woods and mysterious gatherings of crows. In a good example of a simulacrum the light and shadow on the stonework in one of the arches gives the impression of a monk which is there for anyone to see.

Oxfordshire, Hopcrofts Holt Hotel
Many strange incidents at this hotel have been recorded. A Cavalier soldier was seen just outside the building, and a young girl's bed was shaken violently in front of witnesses.

Oxfordshire, near Chipping Norton, The Rollright Stones
This stone circle is said to have healing properties, but on the two occasions when I visited I felt only a very powerful

negative effect from one of the stones, accompanied by pains in the chest and acute nausea.

Suffolk, Borley, the Church
The investigator Harry Price made this village famous by his accounts of mysterious goings-on at the rectory, which was burnt down many years ago. The supernatural manifestations seem to have transferred themselves to the church, and some phantom sounds were recorded on tape in the 1970s. The local population is getting fed up with the behaviour of ghost-hunters.

Warwickshire, Warwick Castle
Both town and castle deserve a visit, especially in summer. The castle's tower is said to be haunted.

The Channel Islands, Jersey
The underground hospital constructed during the German occupation in the Second World War saw many deaths, not only of those constructing the tunnels but also of patients, so it is not surprising that there should be many reports of phantom sightings. I myself had a momentary glimpse of a pile of bodies and limbs and only subsequently noticed that the room in question was labelled 'Morgue'.

SCOTLAND

Culloden Battle Site
Said to be haunted by the ghosts of the fallen.

Glamis Castle
Many legends abound of a monster born to a former owner who grew up hidden away. There is also a floating grey lady.

Loch Ness
This loch is thought to be the home of quite a different type of 'monster'. There have been many sightings, but I failed to see anything. The place is associated with Aleister Crowley who once attempted to summon up the beast.

Cortachy Castle, Angus
The castle is said to be haunted by a ghostly drummer boy and the sound of drumming is supposed to precede a death in the family. The boy was thrown off the battlements to his death stuffed inside his own drum and uttering a curse on the family as he fell.

Nivingston Country Hotel
Guests here have reported ghostly activities at night, including footsteps and doors opening and closing. The shape of an old woman is seen.

Bibliography

J. & C. Bord: *Modern Mysteries of Britain*, Diamond Books 1987.

A. Budden: *Allergies and Aliens*, Redwood Books 1994.

A. Budden: *UFOs. Psychic Close Encounters*, Blandford 1995.

E. Burkes & G. Gibbs: *Ghosthunter*, Headline Books 1995.

S. Gordon: *The Paranormal. An Illustrated Encyclopaedia*, Headline Books 1992.

S. Hapgood: *The World's Greatest Ghost and Poltergeist Stories*, Foulsham 1994.

G. Lyon Playfair: *This House is Haunted*, Souvenir Press 1980.

S. Marsden: *Phantoms of the Isles*, Webb & Bower 1990.

N. Osborne-Thomason: *The Ghost-Hunting Casebook*, Blandford Books 1999.

N. Osborne-Thomason: *Walking through Walls*, Janus 1997.

M. Pipe: *Northamptonshire Ghosts and Legends*, Countryside Books 1993.

E. A. Poe: *Tales of Mystery and Imagination*, Gallery Press 1987.

D. Scott Rogo: *The Return from Silence*, Aquarian 1989.

J. & A. Spencer: *Ghosts and Spirits, Vols. 1 & 2*, Headline Books 2000 and 2001.

R. Wood: *The Widow of Borley*, Gerald Duckworth 1992.

Acknowledgements

No book is ever a solo project. Writers need to draw help and inspiration from those around them. This was particularly true in my case. I would firstly like to thank Bill Simons, a long-standing friend, who helped me find a publisher and believed in me when I didn't believe in myself. Thank you daughter Gemma for your suggestions and Patrick Leonard for accompanying me to many of the interviews and locations. Lastly, thank you to Sevak Gulbekian for suggesting the direction that the book should take and believing in it. Thank you, one and all!

www.clairviewbooks.com

AND THE WOLVES HOWLED
Fragments of two lifetimes
Barbro Karlén
ISBN 1 902636 18 X

LIGHT BEYOND THE DARKNESS
How I healed my suicide son after his death
Doré Deverell
ISBN 1 902636 19 8

LIVING WITH INVISIBLE PEOPLE
A Karmic Autobiography
Jostein Saether
ISBN 1 902636 26 0

A MESSAGE FOR HUMANITY
The Call of God's Angels at a Time of Global Crisis
K. Martin-Kuri
ISBN 1 902636 27 9

MY DESCENT INTO DEATH
and the message of love which brought me back
Howard Storm
ISBN 1 902636 16 3

PSYCHIC WARRIOR
The true story of the CIA's paranormal espionage programme
David Morehouse
ISBN 1 902636 20 1

SEVEN STEPS TO ETERNITY
The true story of one man's journey into the afterlife
as told to 'psychic surgeon' Stephen Turoff
ISBN 1 902636 17 1

WHAT'S BEYOND THAT STAR
A Chronicle of Geomythic Adventure
Richard Leviton
ISBN 1 902636 32 5

WHEN THE STORM COMES
and A MOMENT IN THE BLOSSOM KINGDOM
Barbro Karlén
ISBN 1 902636 23 6

www.clairviewbooks.com